MANDELA

A MAJOR MOTION PICTURE
BASED ON NELSON MANDELA'S BESTSELLING
AUTOBIOGRAPHY *LONG WALK TO FREEDOM*

A FILM AND HISTORICAL COMPANION

Foreword by Ahmed Kathrada

CHRONICLE BOOKS
SAN FRANCISCO

To Madiba

For your leadership and personal sacrifices
in the quest for freedom and democracy in our country.

For your confidence in making me
the custodian of your amazing journey.

For your inspiration and for your friendship.

Anant Singh
Producer, *Mandela*

CONTENTS

FOREWORD

On a cold winter's day in the middle of the filming of *Mandela*, I visited Robben Island, as I have done countless times since my release from prison on October 15, 1989. Later that day I had the privilege of visiting the set of *Mandela* at Cape Town Film Studios, and it was as if I hadn't left the real B Section of Robben Island where I spent eighteen of my twenty-six years of incarceration.

Other parts of the set, such as the Mandela house in Soweto and of course the Palace of Justice—the court in which we were sentenced—were re-created in such great detail that I was immediately transported back in time to the day of our sentencing on June 12, 1964, when Madiba (Nelson Mandela's clan name), Walter Sisulu, Raymond Mhlaba, Govan Mbeki, Denis Goldberg, Elias Motsoaledi, Andrew Mlangeni, and I were sent to prison to start serving out our life sentences. How wonderful it would have been if Walter, Raymond, Govan, and Elias were still alive to see the film or to hold this book in their hands.

It was not long after our release that I met my friend and the producer of the film, Anant Singh. After the preliminary formalities relating to filmmaking were completed, I listened patiently as he told me of his plans to bring the story of *Long Walk to Freedom* to life on the big screen. Today, with the benefit of prison-acquired patience, I feel privileged and delighted to experience his dream now come to fruition. And what a happy coincidence as I write this foreword; I notice that today is May 29, which happens to be Anant's birthday. In his acknowledgment of my message to him, he reminded me that today it is exactly a year and a day since the shooting of the film began.

Mandela is not a story. Part of it is the depiction of a life and lives that many of us lived and experienced together with Madiba. I first met him more than sixty-five years ago. We went through very much together: campaigns, bannings, three major court cases of the 1950s and 1960s, incarceration in prison before our life sentences, and much more.

Yesterday, May 28, 2013, was forty-two years since we in B Section of Robben Island experienced one of the most humiliating moments in prison, which could have ended in unpredictable bloodshed had it not been for our calmness and discipline. It was a Friday night, and very cold. We returned from work, showered, and then were locked up in our individual cells. We did not eat because we were on a hunger strike. After a couple of hours a group of warders, many of them drunk, barged into B Section, unlocked our cells, and ordered us to strip naked and stand facing the wall with our arms in the air. They deliberately took a long time, pretending that they were searching for newspapers (we were only allowed newspapers sixteen years after arriving on the island). It was punishment, and an attempt to break our hunger strike.

We stood shivering but silent. It didn't require any consultation among us, but each of us independently knew that any false move on our part would have been an excuse for the warders to resort to violence. Long experience had taught us that while unplanned and unorganized action can be a simple act of bravado, it can often have severe consequences; we subsequently learnt that they had come to B Section after having indiscriminately and severely assaulted common-law prisoners in their cells. The so-called search had been going on endlessly when Govan Mbeki collapsed. Warders and prisoners alike panicked, knowing that Govan was old and not in good health. We were hurriedly told to dress, and they locked the doors again. Fortunately for us, Govan had not suffered a heart attack. It was the cold and the pressure. Bad as this experience was, coupled with the multiple deprivations and hardships, it failed to crush the optimism and confidence of Robben Islanders.

It is important to acknowledge that while *Mandela* celebrates Madiba's life, he has always been conscious of those who were outside prison, at the coalface of the struggle. And we should always remember that ours was a struggle for a nonracial, nonsexist, democratic South Africa. We should not forget men and women like Vuyisile Mini, Looksmart Ngudle, Solomon Mahlangu, Babla Saloojee, Ahmed Timol, and the hundreds of schoolchildren who were killed in the Soweto uprising of 1976.

Just as important is to remember our white comrades who, too, were part and parcel of the struggle. Many like Ruth Slovo, Neil Aggett, David Webster, and many others did not live to see the democracy for which they gave their lives. Madiba's book *Long Walk to Freedom* makes special mention of Archbishop Desmond Tutu, Albertina Sisulu, Winnie Mandela, the United Democratic Front, and the Congress of South African Trade Unions (COSATU) who were at the forefront of the struggle. Then there are our lawyers. Madiba has always joked that they sent us to jail, but lawyers like Bram Fischer, Vernon Berrange, Joel Joffe, Arthur Chaskalson, and George Bizos, together with international pressure, saved us from the death penalty.

I congratulate Anant and his team: Nilesh Singh and his colleagues at Videovision, director Justin Chadwick, and screenwriter William Nicholson among many others—actors, caterers, drivers, craftspeople, designers, carpenters, cleaners, artists, administrators, and the teams of men and women who have worked tirelessly to make *Mandela* a reality. They come from all walks of life and have all played their part to bring Madiba's story to life.

Finally, a tribute to Geoff Blackwell, Ruth Hobday, and the entire staff at PQ Blackwell for publishing this book and many other books about South Africa. Thank you for being such good friends of the new South Africa.

Ahmed Kathrada
Co-accused in the Defiance Campaign Trial, Treason Trial, and the Rivonia Trial along with Nelson Mandela and other anti-apartheid activists, he spent eighteen years on Robben Island before moving to Pollsmoor Prison for a further seven years. He was released in 1989.

Mandela is led down the steps of his Pretoria residence by his former cellmate Ahmed Kathrada while Graça Machel follows them, on Mandela's eightieth birthday.

PRODUCING MANDELA

My relationship with Nelson Mandela began as a young student activist in apartheid South Africa. He was the symbol of our struggle against the brutal apartheid state. The disparities of the apartheid system had been clear to me even as a ten-year-old. I was acutely aware of the segregation at school, on the beaches, in restaurants, at cinemas, in places of employment, and, indeed, in every facet of our lives. My father, a medical doctor, had a pro bono practice in an African township south of Durban. On the occasions I accompanied him, I was shocked by the appalling conditions that the African people had to endure. It remains a vivid memory for me.

My father introduced me to the silent eight-millimeter films of Charlie Chaplin, Buster Keaton, and others. I was captivated by the moving images, and I am grateful to him for this. On completing my public high-school education, I had aspirations of going to film school, but, of course, the only film school in South Africa was reserved for white people. At that point, two things were at the top of my mind: apartheid and film. In the 1980s Madiba (Nelson Mandela's clan name) and the ANC called for everyone to do what they could to speak out against or fight the oppressive regime. Heeding the call, I made *Place of Weeping*, the first anti-apartheid film shot in South Africa, while I was on the run from the much-feared security police.

Throughout the years, as my career developed in the motion-picture industry, so did my relationships with anti-apartheid activists in South Africa. Nelson Mandela, Walter Sisulu, Ahmed Kathrada, Oliver Tambo, and other anti-apartheid activists portrayed in the film were my heroes.

In 1988 Fatima Meer, a close friend and mentor, wrote *Higher than Hope*, an authorized biography of Nelson Mandela. She gave me the manuscript to read, and I was fascinated by Madiba's story. I immediately realized what an amazing motion picture this would make. Madiba's journey is one that is Capraesque: so full, so dramatic, so romantic, so tragic, and most of all, all for the cause of freedom! Fatima and I had many discussions, until she said, "I am going to visit Nelson and will discuss a film with him." A few weeks

later, she received a handwritten letter from Madiba in prison where he referred to me by name and, in his humble way, questioned the need for a film about his life. That is when it all began—over 25 years ago.

My personal relationship with Madiba began a few weeks after he was released from prison in 1990. I spent about an hour with him at Fatima Meer's house, discussing many issues, including the media, family, motion pictures, globalization, and his life in prison. It was the most fascinating hour I had ever spent with anyone in my entire life. He was charming, and down-to-earth, made me feel important, and wanted to know everything about so many subjects. He had a special charismatic quality and a calming aura around him. This interaction reinforced my passion to make a movie about his journey, and his ever-present modesty and humility left a deep impression on me. I also made the decision to try and assist him in any way possible and to support his initiatives. To this end, when he launched the Nelson Mandela Children's Fund, I became actively involved as a founding donor.

Our relationship became stronger, and I joined him on his international state visits to the United States, United Kingdom, India, and Australia. He also attended the premieres of a number of our films as guest of honor, including *Sarafina!* and the *Cry, the Beloved Country* fundraising premiere in New York, which was hosted by Harvey Weinstein and raised $1.5 million for the Children's Fund.

I am extremely honored that Madiba chose to grant me the coveted and much sought-after film rights to his autobiography, Long Walk to Freedom, especially against aggressive competition. I promised him that I would make the film to the best of my ability, at a time that I believed was right, when the script was ready, and when I had a team together that I firmly believed could do justice to his story. He was totally gracious, and said, "I trust you to do the best you can." I could not have imagined, however, that it would take sixteen years. There were many sceptics who thought it would never happen—I thank all those who have stuck by me over this time.

I hope that this background gives a sense of what this film means to me. As custodian of the film rights, it was my responsibility to convey the morality, power, and strength of Madiba's life story, and to make the film a reality. That responsibility was also shared by everyone involved in the production of the film. We assembled an amazing team including William Nicholson, who had persevered with the script since 1997; Justin Chadwick, whose passion and vision brought a new dimension to the film; Production Designer, Johnny Breedt; and not least of all, the group of outstanding actors. With this formidable unit, and together with my fellow producers, I felt confident as we embarked on the principal photography of *Mandela*. Whilst we encountered many challenges, disappointments, and hardships during production, none were as trying as those endured by Madiba and his colleagues during their decades of incarceration.

We have created a motion picture about one of the most remarkable people in the world. I had complete trust in the team's ability, and I was touched by their steadfast commitment. Together we created a fitting tribute to Madiba and all the activists who suffered so much as they fought for our liberation, under atrocious conditions, never wavering from their sense of integrity, values, humanity, and morality. My sincere gratitude goes out to them for all they have done. Telling this story in two and a half hours cannot do them justice.

Ahmed Kathrada (affectionately known as Kathy), a lifelong friend and confidant of Madiba, visited us at Cape Town Film Studios during pre-production, and he reminded me that May 28, the day we started shooting the film, was one of the darkest days in their lives. It was on that day in 1971 that they were all pulled out of their Robben Island cells at midnight, made to strip, and then humiliated and threatened with violence. This brutal scene is in the film. Kathy has been a steadfast supporter of the film and of me. He has stood by me throughout the past sixteen years, encouraging, motivating and advising me all the way. Without him, we would not have gotten here.

I am thankful for the opportunity to make this film, and in so doing, of enriching the lives of our entire team and those of tens of millions of people all around the world.

During the making of the film we were guided and inspired by the following words by Madiba: "We acknowledge our problems and challenges and then proceed to tackle them with determination and in a spirit of optimism." We have created a film that we hope will inspire people all over the world to uplift themselves and to find the "Mandela" within.

Anant Singh
Producer, *Mandela*

"Anant Singh is a producer I respect very much. Given the resources and backing, he will produce a work of the highest standard and excellence, and it is for that reason I opted for him."

Nelson Mandela, from an interview, Johannesburg, 1996

Ahmed Kathrada, Nelson Mandela, and Anant Singh are photographed together in Los Angeles, California.

DIRECTING MANDELA

I'd just finished directing a Kenyan film, *The First Grader*, when Anant Singh, who was also the producer on the film, talked to me about his plans to produce *Mandela*. Immediately I was concerned. How could you distill such a full life into one film? Madiba's life now spans almost one hundred years of the struggle—one of the most turbulent and well-documented periods in history. To begin to think about turning it into a film was a huge challenge.

I'm not a fan of period movies or biopics, usually finding a veneer between the story and the characters. Anant urged me to read the book, which was a great, informative read, but sprawling in its scope. Anant and William Nicholson, the screenwriter, had been developing the project for years, so I could look at many different drafts of the film script, but I wanted a point of view, a heart to the film. Prior to making *The First Grader*, I had lived and worked in a community in Kenya, and this knowledge informed the film. I spent time teaching at the school I filmed in, and really got to know the people and country I was representing, and the Kenyan man I was depicting. This felt key to me. Being from another country, I was acutely aware that to find the truth I had to listen, learn, and observe the culture and tradition rather than impose my own interpretations upon the film.

The First Grader was opening in Johannesburg. Anant had invited some of Mandela's family and comrades. I was introduced to Ahmed Kathrada, Barbara Hogan, Eddie Daniels, Christo Brandt, Hugh Masekela, Zenani Mandela, and the amazing people who work at the Nelson Mandela Foundation. I wanted to hear about the man. I wanted to discover the intimacy of his family to try and understand the true cost to him as a father and as a husband. I had already amassed a library of biographies, images, DVDs, and books, but I was interested in the man behind the smile and perception we have of him through the history books and politics—the real man.

Beginning with that first visit, and after being taken to Robben Island, Soweto, and Pollsmoor, and meeting family, friends, and comrades and listening to their stories and their personal accounts, it became increasingly clear to me how the film had to be made. It would be a film with a beautiful love story at its heart, but also a film about belief—of never giving up, of being selfless, but strong. This would be the center of the film. My approach connected with Bill and we set to.

Over the next two years I listened to the many stories and points of view from both sides of the struggle. There was an amazing acceptance of me and an openness towards what I was trying to do. The Foundation, rather than being restrictive and overprotective about the Mandela legacy, were totally open. I had complete access to their vaults of research. They were as keen as the filmmakers not to represent Madiba as a deity and an untouchable icon but to create a true account of a man who is just like us, just as flawed—a flesh-and-blood human being.

This freedom flowed into every aspect of the film. Anant had raised the finances for the film almost totally from within South Africa, so we were never answerable to a studio or an outside force who wanted to impose star actors or a way of making the film that fitted the system. I wanted to approach the film as you would do a contemporary drama. I wanted to drop the audience right into the film so that they would believe they were in amongst it, living it with these characters—an experience of being totally submerged in the film. I needed actors who were entirely believable; not look-alikes or sound-alikes but men and women who captured the spirit of the people they were playing.

Shaheen Baig, a casting director I had previously worked with, said she had an instinct that I'd get on with Idris Elba. I'd seen and loved *The Wire*, so I went to meet him in Canada where he was shooting *Pacific Rim*. We spent three days talking, and during that time we realized we had the same intention and that we would, side by side, be making the same film. He just got it—got the way I wanted to approach the material and the man. He is a very brave, instinctive actor, and a good man. After those three days I knew I had what I needed to really begin work on *Mandela*.

Making this film was the single most challenging and fulfilling experience of my life. I met the most amazing people, traveled in a beautiful country, and worked within the most brilliant, vibrant communities. There was a spirit behind the film. It was challenging on every level but ultimately the perfect experience. I'd wake an hour before I needed to because I couldn't wait to get onto set or start what I needed to do.

I have spent the last few years studying a man who has given the world so much, has given me so much, in terms of how he lives his life. I asked production to put Mandela quotes onto each day's call sheet. His words are so powerful—you can live your life by them. The film doesn't attempt to tell the whole story, but I hope it catches some of the spirit and love and acceptance that I have felt in making it.

Justin Chadwick
Director, *Mandela*

Justin Chadwick talks with Idris Elba during filming of *Mandela*.

DESIGNING MANDELA

About fifteen years ago I was asked if I would be interested in working on the film *Long Walk to Freedom*. Initially, I was offered the task of being responsible for the action vehicles, and although this was not the job description I had hoped for, I was nevertheless happy to be involved in the project. Little did I know at the time that this project would go full circle for me, and I would eventually become the production designer on *Mandela*.

After a number of years had passed, Anant Singh approached me to design the film. My initial involvement was to do a budget, a feasibility study on locations and historical references, and other related research. Anant wanted to ensure that the production design was as authentic as possible and so retained my services in 2007, long before the film went into production. This long duration meant that my research was able to be extensive and detailed.

The momentum increased in 2010 when I began working in earnest on this project. I also spent a great deal of time location scouting for the Mandela film. Without a firm official start date, it was extremely difficult for me to hold on to crew, and as people moved on to other projects during the hiatus periods, I had to start again from scratch. I knew that things were serious when Anant contacted each crew member individually and assured them that we were starting the film very soon. This enabled me to retain the core group that I needed.

Director Justin Chadwick and I had met previously when he was looking for a production designer for his film *The First Grader*. We immediately connected. It also meant that when *Mandela* came along, we already knew each other and had a good synergy.

Justin and I started out by looking for possible locations for the film. As I had done quite a few fact-finding scouting missions prior to him coming on board, we were able to eliminate a number of areas, saving us time during preproduction.

Areas scouted fifteen years before no longer existed or had been modernized. Many of the real places where events had taken place had been turned into museums or heritage sites, or had simply been abandoned. This made our task a lot more difficult, but the final result was that we came across a great deal of very interesting new possibilities. Of course we were still able to shoot in some of the real locations, and we did this wherever it made practical, logistical, or aesthetic sense.

We wanted to create a visceral world which the actors could simply drop into and perform in—a world that would be realistic enough that it would almost go unnoticed by the cast and crew. On empty locations I always try to find an existing structure—even a dead tree or something as simple as a fence—as this provides a foundation from which to build, thus creating a truly organic "feel" to the environment.

On *Mandela* I had the pleasurable challenge of creating amazing sets on sound-stages at Cape Town Film Studios and on the studio's backlot. The construction, scenics, props, set-decoration, and greens departments were made up of a talented group of almost one thousand people who were able to finish off the set pieces with convincing authenticity.

Some of the real locations provided other challenges and it was the art department's task to come up with solutions to these problems. For example, Robben Island was logistically impossible to shoot as it is visited daily by thousands of tourists, and the Palace of Justice in Pretoria is still used as a working court.

With the Palace of Justice, a full-scale replica of the entire courtroom was built with such detail that it is difficult to tell it apart from the real courtroom. Building the replica gave the director the creative freedom to set up shots as he required, the most amazing being a Steadicam shot that followed the Rivonia Trialists from the holding cell, down a corridor, up the stairs into the courtroom, and finally into the dock, without a single cut.

This film was by far the biggest undertaking by an art department on any film shot in South Africa. For me, it was vital to have the right crew on board from day one, and together we were fortunate enough to build some of the biggest set pieces ever built in South Africa. We are delighted that Anant has decided to donate some of these sets to the Nelson Mandela Museum in Qunu which will ensure that they are preserved for posterity.

Not only were the sets a huge undertaking for the art department, but we also used a total of three hundred and fifty action vehicles on the production, a first in our industry. If you consider that this includes cars from the early 1920s, spanning every decade right up to the 1990s, I sincerely doubt that this achievement could ever be equalled.

It has been an absolute privilege for me and everyone in the art department to work on a film about Nelson Mandela and a period of history that we lived through, and an honor to showcase Mandela's inspirational life story to the rest of the world.

Johnny Breedt
Production Designer, *Mandela*

Johnny Breedt stands in front of one of the huts created for the set of *Mandela*.

INTRODUCTION

In the summer of 1996 Nelson Mandela presented Anant Singh with the film rights to his autobiography, *Long Walk to Freedom*. Anant then came to me with the suggestion that I write the screenplay for the film. I had worked with Anant before, as the screenwriter of *Sarafina!*, and the collaboration had been a happy one. *Long Walk to Freedom* was something else.

I knew from the first that the project was too important to get wrong, and that it was bigger than me. Mandela's story transcended the man and his country. Here was the real-life evidence that a brutally oppressed people could overthrow their masters, could win their freedom, could achieve power in their own land, and could do all this by other means than armed revolution. All history to this point had taught us the lesson that no regime surrenders power voluntarily; that there must be a war of liberation. The American Revolution, the French Revolution, and the Russian Revolution all cemented in our minds the legend of righteous violence. Then came Gandhi with his radical creed of nonviolence, but his oppressor, the British Empire, was already on the retreat. Nelson Mandela grew up in a country ruled by a white minority that had nowhere to go. That minority believed that if the black majority ever gained power, they, the nation's rulers, would lose everything: their power, their property, their lives. Such a stark conflict of interests could surely only ever be settled by civil war, a war to the bitter end. And of course there was war of a kind in South Africa. Many died. But in place of the bloodbath so often prophesied, a miracle took place. Realizing that apartheid rule could no longer continue, the white minority government surrendered its power. The government formed after the first free elections included both white and black leaders. Confrontation gave way to collaboration. The seductive glamour of violence was trumped by the gentler power of forgiveness. People on both sides of the divide showed themselves capable of choosing peace over war, love over hate.

This then is a story about the fundamentals of human nature. It's a profoundly optimistic story. And it all really happened.

Knowing this, I put it to Anant that the film should be written by a South African. I hadn't grown up in the townships, or even in the privileged enclaves of white South Africa. What right did I have to tell the story? Anant replied, "This is a story for the world."

I began planning the research in late 1996. Looking back over the years, I find one of the very first notes I wrote outlining my approach:

> *Mandela has extraordinary powers of hope and forgiveness. When such a man achieves complete victory at the end, it is also a victory for all that is best in us.*

My first research trip took me to Robben Island in the company of Ahmed Kathrada, Mandela's fellow prisoner there, and on to Pollsmoor Prison, and then to Victor Verster Prison, where Mandela spent his final years in captivity. On the road back, our car, carrying Kathrada, Anant, and myself, spun out of control and crashed into a rock. I was injured (my nose broken and shoulder dislocated), Anant suffered whiplash, but Kathrada, thankfully, was unhurt. One result of this accident was that I was unable to meet Mandela as planned. By the time I was back in South Africa, with the first draft already written, I had become aware of how burdensome it was to Mandela to be forever meeting strangers, forever posing for photographs for other people's souvenirs. So I did not press for a meeting. The truth was I had already met him. I had begun to bring to life the Mandela of our film. He is not the same being as the real man, and never can be. But when shown a section of the finished film—the glorious final shot of the old man walking in the Transkei where he grew up as a child—Mandela said, "Is that me?" So I dare to hope we've got close.

The work of creating my Mandela proved far harder than I had anticipated. I calculate that between 1996 and now I've written thirty-three different drafts. Had I known that I'd still be working on the project sixteen years later I may not have had the heart to continue. But of course with each draft we all believed we were a few months away from starting production.

Why did it take so long? Because Mandela's life—the politics of his struggle and his personal journey—involves so many and such complex issues. What to keep in and what to leave out? Where to start? Where to finish? And how could we ever fit it all into a span of two hours or so?

I began my first draft with a scene in the Palace of Versailles in 1918. A delegation arrives in the grand Hall of Mirrors, where the victorious powers are dictating the terms of peace at the end of the First World War. The delegation consists of five black leaders from the South African Native National Congress, which was to become the African National Congress (ANC). They have come in response to US President Woodrow Wilson's ringing declaration that the recent peace guarantees justice and freedom to all the peoples of the world. The black delegation's appeal for their own justice and freedom is laughingly dismissed by a minor official: "It's sweet, really. Like children playing at mommies and daddies." I intended this shocking scene to give a measure of how far the cause of black liberation had to travel. Also, 1918 was the year of Mandela's birth.

That first draft, dated July 4, 1997, ended with Mandela's release from prison. Over the years the Versailles opening was dropped, and the story was extended to cover the tumultuous period leading up to South Africa's first free elections. Other than that, I find that the structure I created right from the start has remained surprisingly constant.

But it's been a bumpy ride. I realize now that we could never have pushed through that first script. All our supporters in South Africa, those who had lived and suffered with Mandela, needed to make the journey with us. That first draft was sent to Kathrada, gentlest and wisest of men, and of course a main character in our film. My screenplay drew from him a long list of queries, corrections, and objections; in particular his fear that I was being disrespectful to Mandela. My letter in response, dated August 18, 1997, runs in part:

The great challenge in work of this kind is to bring the story to life. This comes down to the presentation of central characters whom the audience cares about. Those film biographies that fail, almost always do so because the makers have been too reverent. The ones that succeed do so by humanizing their heroes, showing them to be vulnerable. Against such a background, their achievements then win our love and sympathy. In the case of Mandela, his extraordinary stoicism and endurance will always be admirable, but I'm reaching that little bit further, to touch the heart. And to do that, we have to sense how much he suffered and how great a price he has paid. I have taken his marriages as a major theme, because through this side of his life so many people will be able to identify themselves with him. Very few have endured long prison sentences. Many have known the anguish of failed marriages: of loving and losing love, of feeling the guilt of failing loved ones. My belief is that the more human Mandela becomes to us, the more extraordinary and admirable his achievements become. Like you, I see Mandela as a role model, but I do not see him as a saint. If he is superhuman, his qualities are beyond our reach. If he is human, then we too can say, "As he did, so can I." That is the true role model.

Kathrada has been our staunchest supporter throughout this long process. I have attended to his every criticism, and he in turn has come to tolerate the necessary simplifications of filmmaking. But the long delay and the many drafts are only partly due to the difficulty of telling the story. All films are group endeavors. Several elements must come together before the cameras can roll: there must be an agreed screenplay, a director, suitable actors, and financiers willing to risk large sums of money. For every movie it proves hard to line up all these elements at the same time. The usual order is as follows: the screenplay attracts the director; the screenplay and director combined attract the star actor; the screenplay, director, and star actor attract the finance. On this project we have over the years gone some distance with at least five directors and as many star actors, but problems of availability, or uncertainty over the screenplay, or competing projects have caused each plan to founder.

Back in my files, I find this memo sent in response to our then director, who was concerned that I was failing to focus the story:

I ask about every movie: Who is the central character? What does he want? And what makes me want it too? A movie that successfully answers this question works. That seems to me to be the major task before me in this rewrite. It's not a subtle or complex point; it's not hard for any of us to understand. It's entirely about emotion. It won't be solved by more research, or more insights into the political process, or more revelations about Mandela's true nature. It can only be solved in the age-old way of drama, by making us care about the central character: love him, suffer with him, triumph with him. If I can achieve this, you'll find all your other concerns will melt away.

You raise the issue of the scope of the story. Are we attempting to tell too much? Would we get a more subtle and moving film by focusing on a part of Mandela's life only? My own answer is no, the whole sweep of his life is part of the power of his story and magnitude of his achievement. You ask, on what basis do we choose what to keep and what to leave out? My answer is we choose what makes us feel for Mandela. We go for the emotion. We are making a film about a man born to an oppressed race, who made the decision to give his life and his chance of love and happiness to fight that oppression, and who triumphed in the end. Why do we care about this? Because it's a David and Goliath story. Because it's right against might. Because it helps us to believe that humanity and dignity can outlast hatred and violence. But most of all because we love the hero and want to see him win.

That director in the end moved on to other projects, as is common in the film world. But his rigorous questioning of the screenplay left a valuable mark, as did that of many others over the years. In order to solve the problem of what to leave in and what to leave out, we experimented with different starting points: the little boy in the Transkei hills, the young man who made the decision to take up violence, the prisoner arriving at Robben Island. We experimented with breaking up the time sequence and with using flashbacks. At the urging of one director, we added an entire end section that took the story on to 1994. That director, too, moved on to another project, but his instinct proved invaluable. As I struggled to compress the political complexity of the years after Mandela's release into a few pages of script, I realized that these few years witnessed not only the election of South Africa's first-ever black president, but also the public end of Mandela's marriage to Winnie Mandela. At this point, one simple fact about the story jumped out at me and caused me to see the entire screenplay in a new way.

Mandela and Winnie's love story—their love tragedy—was itself a metaphor for the struggle for freedom. Through their parallel lives we could represent the two paths to liberation: Mandela isolated on Robben Island, learning to forgive; Winnie tortured beyond endurance, learning to hate. They loved each other. They were driven apart.

All the pieces were already there before me. It was simply a matter of adjusting the emphasis. The new end section allowed me to play out the relationship to its sad end. I gave Mandela one simple, terrible line that said it all: "What they have done to my wife is their only victory over me." And there it was, everything we'd always wanted: a great victory accompanied by great personal defeat; a hero who's human, who can be hurt; a personal, emotional journey that is also the story of a nation.

Quite suddenly, hardly able to believe it ourselves, we had a film ready to shoot. All we needed was a director and a star. After so many false starts, the gods smiled on us, and the elements lined up: director Justin Chadwick entered our lives like a fireball, exploding with a brilliant energy, making the screenplay his own. He immersed himself in the world of Soweto and Robben Island, in the voices and songs of South Africa, and breathed a rich and vibrant life into every scene. And, most crucially of all, he went looking for his star, and he found Idris Elba. It all now looks inevitable—who else but Idris could have given us the charisma, the majesty, the humanity of Nelson Mandela? But the stack of drafts now gathering dust on my shelves reminds me that it's been a long journey.

Our film is not a full historical record. How can it be, in little more than two hours? It tries to pass on to the next generation the extraordinary achievement of a man who dared to forgive his enemies. It tries to make people who have never heard of apartheid and care nothing for South Africa care about this one man and what he came to stand for. I suppose it is, in its way, the creation of a legend. But the legend is true.

William Nicholson
Screenwriter, *Mandela*

William Nicholson on the set of *Mandela*.

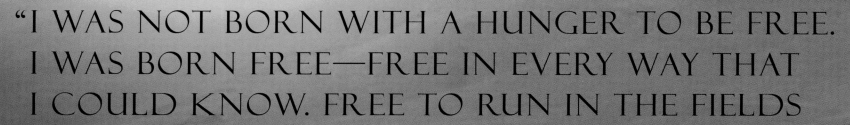

"I WAS NOT BORN WITH A HUNGER TO BE FREE. I WAS BORN FREE—FREE IN EVERY WAY THAT I COULD KNOW. FREE TO RUN IN THE FIELDS near my mother's hut, free to swim in the clear stream that ran through my village, free to roast mealies under the stars and ride the broad backs of slow-moving bulls. As long as I obeyed my father and abided by the customs of my tribe, I was not troubled by the laws of man or God."

Nelson Mandela, from *Long Walk to Freedom*, 1994

Apart from life, a strong constitution, and an abiding connection to the Thembu royal house, the only thing my father bestowed upon me at birth was a name, Rolihlahla. In Xhosa, Rolihlahla literally means "pulling the branch of a tree," but its colloquial meaning is "troublemaker."

I was born on July 18, 1918, at Mvezo, a tiny river on the banks of the Mbashe River in the district of Umtata, the capital of Transkei. My father, Gadla Henry Mphakanyiswa, was a chief by both blood and custom. He was confirmed as chief of Mvezo by the king of the Thembu tribe, though under British rule his selection had to be ratified by the government.

According to tradition, the Thembu people migrated from the Drakensberg mountains in the sixteenth century, where they were incorporated into the Xhosa nation. Each Xhosa belongs to a clan that traces its descent back to a specific forefather. I am a member of the Madiba clan, named after a Thembu chief who ruled in the Transkei in the eighteenth century.

Right and pages 16, 17, and 18–19: Mandela's childhood in the Transkei province in the Eastern Cape is brought to life in the film.

My father had four wives, the third of whom was my mother, Nosekeni Fanny, the daughter of Nkedama from the amaMpemvu clan of the Xhosa. My father sired thirteen children in all, four boys and nine girls, and I am the youngest son.

"YOU ARE MY FIRST-BORN, THE JOY OF MY HEART. MAKE ME PROUD OF YOU."

The character Nosekeni Fanny, Nelson Mandela's mother, from the film *Mandela*

When I was an infant, my father was involved in a dispute that deprived him of his chieftainship. One day, he asserted his traditional prerogative as a chief and challenged the authority of the magistrate over some tribal matter. Such behavior was regarded as the height of insolence. The magistrate simply deposed my father, thus ending the Mandela family chieftainship. As a result, my father, who was a wealthy nobleman by the standards of his time, lost both his fortune and his title. My mother then moved to Qunu, north of Mvezo, where she would have the support of friends and relations.

From an early age, I spent most of my time in the veld playing and fighting with the other boys of the village. We were mostly left to our own devices. We played with toys we made ourselves, molding animals and birds out of clay and building ox-drawn sledges out of tree branches.

My mother became a Christian and I was baptized into the Methodist Church and sent to school. On the first day of school my teacher, Miss Mdingane, gave each of us an English name as was the custom among Africans in those days. That day, Miss Mdingane told me that my new name was Nelson.

"IT IS WHAT WE MAKE OUT OF WHAT WE HAVE, NOT WHAT WE ARE GIVEN, THAT SEPARATES ONE PERSON FROM ANOTHER."

Nelson Mandela, from *Long Walk to Freedom*, 1994

> ## "THE ACTING KING WHO BROUGHT ME UP WAS APPOINTED, WAS ELECTED, ACTING PARAMOUNT CHIEF BY THE TRIBE AS A RESULT OF THE INFLUENCE OF MY FATHER."
>
> Nelson Mandela, from a conversation with Richard Stengel, March 10, 1993

When I was twelve years old my father died, and my mother informed me that I would be leaving Qunu.

We traveled in silence until the sun was sinking slowly towards the horizon. Late in the afternoon we came upon a village at the center of which was a large and gracious home consisting of two houses and seven stately *rondavels* (huts), surrounded by spacious gardens. This was the Great Place, Mqhekezweni, the provisional capital of Thembuland, the royal residence of Regent Jongintaba Dalindyebo, acting king of the Thembu people.

I learned later that, after my father's death, Jongintaba had offered to become my guardian. He would treat me as he treated his other children, and I would have the same advantages as they.

If the world of Mqhekezweni revolved around the regent, my smaller world revolved around his two children. Justice, the elder, was his only son and heir to the Great Place, and Nomafu was the regent's daughter. I lived with them and was treated exactly as they were.

Above: Jongintaba, chief regent of the Thembu people, was appointed guardian of the young Mandela by his dying father.

Right: A scene from the film in which villagers gather for the opportunity to air their grievances before the chief.

"LOOK ON THE FLOWER OF THE XHOSA NATION! THEY ARE YOUNG, AND STRONG, AND BEAUTIFUL! THEIR CHILDHOOD IS OVER!"

A praise song from the film *Mandela*

Right: Young Thembu initiates in 1930.

Far right and following page: Recreations from the film of young men from the tribe as they undergo their initiation to manhood. Initiation included the ritual of circumcision.

When I was sixteen, the regent decided that it was time I became a man. In Xhosa tradition, this is achieved through one means only: circumcision. An uncircumcised male cannot marry or officiate in tribal rituals. It is not just a surgical procedure, but a lengthy and elaborate ritual in preparation for manhood.

Early in the new year, we journeyed to two grass huts in a secluded valley on the banks of the Mbashe River, known as Tyhalarha, the traditional place of circumcision for Thembu kings. The huts were seclusion lodges, where we were to live isolated from society. At the end of our seclusion, a great ceremony was held to welcome us as men to society. Our families, friends, and local chiefs gathered for speeches, songs, and gift-giving.

The main speaker was Chief Meligqili, the son of Dalindyebo. He began by remarking how fine it was that we were continuing a long tradition. Then his tone suddenly changed. "There sit our sons," he said.

"The flower of the Xhosa tribe, the pride of our nation. We have just circumcised them in a ritual that promises them manhood, but it is a promise that can never be fulfilled. For we Xhosa, and all black South Africans, are a conquered people. We are slaves in our own country. We are tenants in our own soil. We have no strength, no power, no control over our own destiny in the land of our birth. Among these young men are chiefs who will never rule because we have no power to govern ourselves; soldiers who will never fight for we have no weapons to fight with; scholars who will never teach because we have no place for them to study. The abilities, the intelligence, the promise of these young men will be squandered in their attempt to eke out a living doing the simplest, most mindless chores for the white man. These gifts today are naught, for we cannot give them the greatest gift of all, which is freedom and independence."

Without exactly understanding why, his words began to work on me. He had sown a seed, and though I let that seed lie dormant for a long season, it eventually began to grow.

"BUT IF I HAD STAYED AT HOME I WOULD HAVE BEEN A RESPECTED CHIEF TODAY, YOU KNOW? AND I WOULD HAVE HAD A BIG STOMACH AND A LOT OF CATTLE AND SHEEP."

Nelson Mandela, from a conversation with Richard Stengel, May 3, 1993

At the end of my second year at Fort Hare, the regent summoned Justice and me to a meeting. "My children," he said in a very somber tone, "I fear that I am not much longer for this world, and before I journey to the land of the ancestors, it is my duty to see my two sons properly married. I have, accordingly, arranged unions for both of you."

I could not go through with this marriage, which I considered unfair and ill-advised. At the same time, I could no longer remain under the regent's guidance if I rejected his plan for me. Justice agreed, and the two of us decided that the only choice remaining was to run away to Johannesburg.

Right: Mandela in his first suit given to him by the regent when he went to Clarkebury Boarding Institute in 1934. After Clarkebury, he went on to Healdtown College and then to Fort Hare, the only black university in South Africa and the Alma Mater of the revolution to come. He was expelled after embarking on protest action for improved student rights.

Far right: Mandela on the roof of Kholvad House, Johannesburg, 1953.

Arriving at about ten o'clock that evening, we saw before us, glinting in the distance, a maze of lights that seemed to stretch in all directions. I was terribly excited to see the city I had heard about since I was a child. Johannesburg had always been depicted as a city of dreams, a city of danger, and of opportunity. It was the city of gold where I would soon be making my home. I had reached the end of what seemed like a long journey, but it was actually the very beginning of a much longer and more trying journey that would test me in ways I could not then have imagined.

Above: Johannesburg, 1941.

Left: Johannesburg in the 1940s is brought to life in the film. Idris Elba, as Nelson Mandela, is seen emerging from the gym.

L azar Sidelsky had agreed to take me on as a clerk while I completed my bachelor of arts degree. To that end, I was studying at night with UNISA, the University of South Africa. As a combination of a clerk and a messenger, I would find, arrange, and file documents and serve or deliver papers around Johannesburg.

Life in Alexandra was exhilarating and precarious. It was desperately overcrowded; every square foot was occupied by either a ramshackle house or a tin-roofed shack. Police raids were a regular feature of life in Alexandra.

"LIFE WAS CHEAP AND THE GUN AND THE KNIFE RULED AT NIGHT."

Nelson Mandela, from his unpublished autobiographical manuscript, written on Robben Island, 1975

Above left: Mandela found accommodation in Alexandra, a crowded but vibrant slum known as "Dark City," because it had no electricity, about six miles north of the downtown center. He lived in a corrugated-iron shack with a dirt floor and no running water.

Above right: Upon receiving his BA and while still working as an articled clerk, Mandela began studying for a law degree at the University of the Witwatersrand. There, he was introduced to a new world of political and social ideas, meeting many people who would later play significant roles in the struggle to end apartheid.

Left: Shebeens, or illicit bars, sprung up in many black townships as blacks were not permitted in whites-only drinking establishments. This image from the film of a shebeen in Sophiatown conveys the lively atmosphere created by the music and dancing that took place in shebeens, which were also important places for discussions on politics and social issues. Actress Nomfusi Gotyana plays singer and civil rights activist Miriam Makeba.

W alter Sisulu's name was becoming prominent as both a businessman and a local leader. Despite his youth, he seemed to me an experienced man of the world. Sisulu's office specialized in properties for Africans. In the 1940s, there were still quite a few areas where freehold properties could be purchased by Africans, smallholdings located in such places as Alexandra and Sophiatown. In some of these areas, Africans had owned their own homes for several generations.

Above left: Walter Sisulu, a staunch member of the African National Congress, played an important role in shaping Mandela's political ideals. It was Sisulu who introduced Mandela to Lazar Sidelsky, a white lawyer from the firm Witkin, Sidelsky, and Eidelman, who believed black people should be treated as equals and employed Mandela as an articled clerk.

Above right: Mandela often relieved stress by boxing. He was intrigued by the sport, viewing it as more about strategy than a display of violent strength, and the fancy footwork he learned in the ring was to stand him in good stead in the political arena.

Right: Idris Elba, playing Nelson Mandela, is seen sparring with an opponent while Tony Kgoroge, as Walter Sisulu, looks on.

"SO LET'S DEFY THEIR UNJUST LAWS! WHAT CAN THEY DO? IMPRISON US ALL? LET THEM! THEN, WHEN ALL OF US ARE IN PRISON, LET THEM MINE THEIR OWN GOLD, AND CLEAN THEIR OWN HOUSES, AND WASH THEIR OWN CLOTHES!"

The character Nelson Mandela, from the film *Mandela*

I cannot pinpoint a moment when I became politicized, when I knew that I would spend my life in the liberation of struggle. I had no epiphany, no singular revelation, no moment of truth, but a steady accumulation of a thousand slights and a thousand indignities produced in me an anger, a desire to fight the system that imprisoned my people.

Other young men were thinking along the same lines and we would all meet to discuss these ideas. The general consensus was that some action must be taken, and forming a Youth League was proposed as a way of lighting a fire under the leadership of the ANC.

Above: Mandela was one of the founding members of the ANC Youth League in 1944.

Left: Idris Elba, in his portrayal of Nelson Mandela as a law clerk, is seen here being castigated by a white magistrate.

Walter's house in Orlando was my home away from home. The house was always full, and there was a perpetual discussion going on about politics. It was there that I met Evelyn Mase, my first wife. She was a quiet, pretty girl who did not seem overawed by the comings and goings at the Sisulus'. I asked Evelyn out very soon after our first meeting. Within a few months I had asked her to marry me, and she accepted.

Early in 1946, Evelyn and I moved to a two-room municipal house of our own in Orlando East and thereafter to a slightly larger house at No. 8115 Orlando West. That year our first son, Madiba Thembekile, was born. He was given my clan name of Madiba, but was known by the nickname Thembi.

Above: In this photograph of Walter and Albertina Sisulu's wedding in 1944, Mandela is on the far left while Evelyn Mase, his future wife, stands next to him. They were married a few months later and had four children together.

Left: Idris Elba, as Nelson Mandela, meets with Tony Kgoroge as Walter Sisulu, Tshallo Chokwe as Oliver Tambo, and Riaad Moosa as Ahmed Kathrada at Sisulu's house in Orlando in this scene from the film, one of the many regular meetings held by Mandela and his comrades.

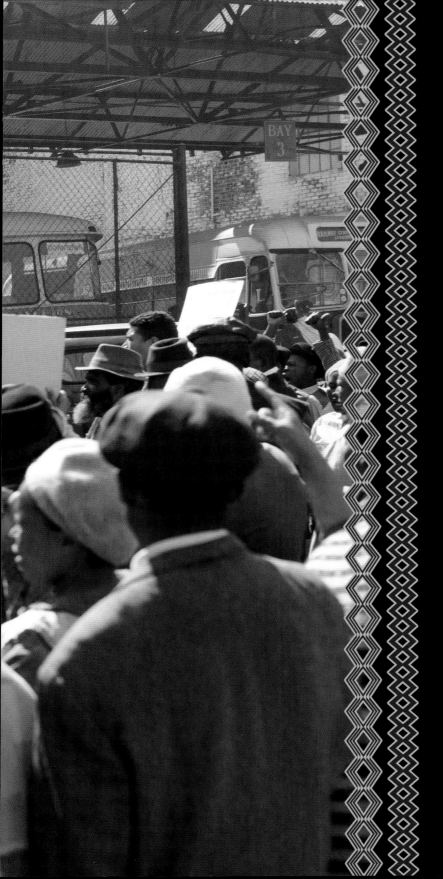

"MAKE ME PROUD OF YOU, NELSON. SHOW THEM AN AFRICAN CAN DO AS WELL AS A WHITE MAN. SHOW THEM AN AFRICAN CAN HAVE HIS OWN LAW FIRM."

The character Lazar Sidelsky, from the film *Mandela*

In August 1943 I marched with ten thousand others in support of the Alexandra bus boycott, a protest against the raising of fares from four pence to five. This campaign had a great effect on me. In a small way, I had departed from my role as an observer and had become a participant. I found that to march with one's people was exhilarating and inspiring. But I was also impressed by the boycott's effectiveness: after nine days, during which the buses ran empty, the company reinstated the fare to four pence.

In 1947 I was elected to the executive committee of the Transvaal ANC, and in August 1952 I opened my own law office and I asked Oliver Tambo to join me. We were not the only African lawyers in South Africa, but we were the only firm of African lawyers.

Left: Mandela inside the offices of Mandela and Tambo, the first all-African law firm in the country.

Right: Oliver Tambo, with his quiet, calm demeanor, made an ideal partner to Mandela's charismatic courtroom personality.

Far left: In this recreation from the film, Tony Kgoroge, as Walter Sisulu, and a fellow activist address a large crowd at the Alexandra bus depot to protest against the raising of bus fares.

"I WANT AT ONCE TO MAKE IT CLEAR THAT I AM NO RACIALIST, AND I DETEST RACIALISM, BECAUSE I REGARD IT AS A BARBARIC THING, WHETHER IT COMES FROM A BLACK MAN OR FROM A WHITE MAN."

Nelson Mandela, from an application for the recusal of the magistrate Mr. W. A. van Helsdingen,
Old Synagogue, Pretoria, South Africa, October 22, 1962

Africans could not vote, but that did not mean we did not care who won elections. In the white general election of 1948 the Nationalists were led to victory by Dr. Daniel Malan. Malan's platform was known as apartheid. Apartheid was a new term but an old idea. It literally means "apartness."

In March 1951 Walter Sisulu broached the idea to a small group of us of a national civil disobedience campaign. He outlined a plan under which selected volunteers from all groups would deliberately invite imprisonment by defying certain laws.

Above: Racial discrimination in South Africa was ever-present, as depicted in this image from the film.

Right: Idris Elba, as Nelson Mandela, and his companion are stopped for a pass check by a white policeman.

On May 31, 1952, the executives of the ANC announced that the Defiance Campaign would begin on June 26. Two stages of defiance were proposed. In the first stage, a small number of well-trained volunteers would break selected laws in a handful of urban areas. They would enter proscribed areas without permits, use Whites Only facilities such as toilets, Whites Only railway compartments, waiting rooms, and post-office entrances. The second stage was envisioned as mass defiance, accompanied by strikes and industrial actions across the country.

On that first day of the Defiance Campaign more than 250 volunteers around the country violated various unjust laws and were imprisoned. It was an auspicious beginning. Over the next five months, 8,500 people took part in the campaign.

On July 30, 1952, I was arrested with twenty others under the charge of violation of the Suppression of Communism Act. On December 2, we were all found guilty of "statutory communism" and were sentenced to nine months' imprisonment with hard labor, but the sentence was suspended for two years.

"THE CAMPAIGN FREED ME FROM ANY LINGERING SENSE OF DOUBT OR INFERIORITY I MIGHT STILL HAVE FELT;

it liberated me from the feeling of being overwhelmed by the power and seeming invincibility of the white man and his institutions. But now the white man had felt the power of my punches and I could walk upright like a man, and look everyone in the eye with the dignity that comes from not having succumbed to oppression and fear. I had come of age as a freedom fighter."

Nelson Mandela, from *Long Walk to Freedom*, 1994

Right: Protests held across the country as part of the Defiance Campaign are brought to life in the film.

Situated four miles west of Johannesburg's center was the African township of Sophiatown. In Johannesburg, the Western Areas Removal scheme meant the evacuation of Sophiatown. The government was callously planning on relocating all Sophiatown's African residents to another black township.

In the hazy dawn hours of February 9, 1955, four thousand police and army troops cordoned off the township while workers razed empty houses and government trucks began moving families from Sophiatown.

"THE BOERS CALL SOPHIATOWN A SLUM. ALL THE PEOPLE WHO HAVE HOMES THERE ARE TO BE EVICTED BY FORCE. SOPHIATOWN IS TO BE BULLDOZED, SO THEY CAN BUILD HOUSES FOR THE RICH. WELL, LET THEM TRY!"

The character Nelson Mandela, from the film *Mandela*

Above left: Protests in Sophiatown against the government's forced removals, 1953.

Above right: The destruction of Sophiatown happened over the course of five years. The scheduled date to begin removals was February 12, 1955, but three days earlier two thousand armed police invaded the area and forced families out of their homes.

Left: A recreation of the destruction of Sophiatown after bulldozers have passed through the township.

"I WAS THIRTY-FIVE, AND HENCEFORTH, ALL MY ACTIONS AND PLANS ON BEHALF OF THE ANC AND THE LIBERATION STRUGGLE WOULD BECOME SECRET AND ILLEGAL."

Nelson Mandela, from *Long Walk to Freedom*, 1994

In Johannesburg, I had become a man of the city. I wore smart suits, drove an Oldsmobile, and commuted daily to a downtown office. In September 1955, as my banning orders had ended, I decided to take advantage of my freedom and get some respite from the city. I took on a case in the little *dorp* of Villiers in the Orange Free State.

I found a group of policemen waiting to serve me with an order under the Suppression of Communism Act requiring me to resign from the ANC, restricting me to the Johannesburg district, and prohibiting me from attending any meetings or gatherings for two years.

Right: Idris Elba portrays Nelson Mandela as a lawyer in the film *Mandela*.

In the mid-1950s my marriage to Evelyn had begun to unravel. My devotion to the ANC and the struggle was unremitting. This disturbed Evelyn. She had always assumed that politics was a youthful diversion, that I would someday return to the Transkei and practice there as a lawyer. We had many arguments about this, and I patiently explained to her that politics was not a distraction but my lifework, and that it was an essential part of my being. She could not accept this. I never lost my respect and admiration for her, but in the end we could not make our marriage work.

One afternoon, I drove a friend to the medical school at the University of the Witwatersrand. As I passed a bus stop, I noticed out of the corner of my eye a lovely young woman waiting for the bus. I was struck by her beauty, and I turned my head to get a better look at her. Her name was Nomzamo Winifred Madikizela, known as Winnie. She was working as the first black female social worker at Baragwanath Hospital. The moment I first glimpsed Winnie Nomzamo, I knew that I wanted to have her as my wife.

Above, right, and following page: Idris Elba and Naomie Harris portray Nelson and Winnie's courtship and wedding in the film.

Shortly after I filed for divorce from Evelyn, I told Winnie she should have a fitting for a wedding dress and suggested she inform her parents that she was to be married.

The wedding took place on June 14, 1958. I applied for a relaxation of my banning orders and was given six days' leave of absence from Johannesburg.

Above: Nelson and Winnie on their wedding day in 1958. Mandela was granted a temporary stay of a five-year banning order restricting him to Johannesburg so that the wedding could be held in Winnie's native Pondoland.

"I WOULD HOPE THAT THE AVERAGE INDIVIDUAL EXPERIENCES ONE OF THE HIGHEST LEVELS OF EMOTIONAL ATTACHMENTS, SATISFACTION, AND HAPPINESS WHEN IN LOVE."

Nelson Mandela, from a personal file, date unknown

Sharpeville was a small township about thirty-five miles south of Johannesburg. In the early afternoon, a crowd of several thousand surrounded the police station in an anti-pass demonstration. The demonstrators were controlled and unarmed. The police force of seventy-five was greatly outnumbered and panicky. No one heard warning shots or an order to shoot, but suddenly the police opened fire on the crowd and continued to shoot as the demonstrators turned and ran in fear. When the area had cleared, sixty-nine Africans lay dead, most of them shot in the back as they were fleeing.

"IN 1960, THERE WAS A SHOOTING AT SHARPEVILLE, WHICH RESULTED IN THE PROCLAMATION OF A STATE OF EMERGENCY AND THE DECLARATION OF THE ANC AS AN UNLAWFUL ORGANIZATION. MY COLLEAGUES AND I, AFTER CAREFUL CONSIDERATION, DECIDED THAT WE WOULD NOT OBEY THIS DECREE."

Nelson Mandela, speech from the dock, Rivonia Trial, Palace of Justice, Pretoria, South Africa, April 20, 1964

Left: The mass funeral for the Sharpeville victims, 1960. Police fired over 700 shots into the crowd during the massacre in which 69 people were killed and 180 people, including children, were wounded.

Far left: This dramatic recreation of the Sharpeville massacre conveys the terror as demonstrators attempt to flee from police.

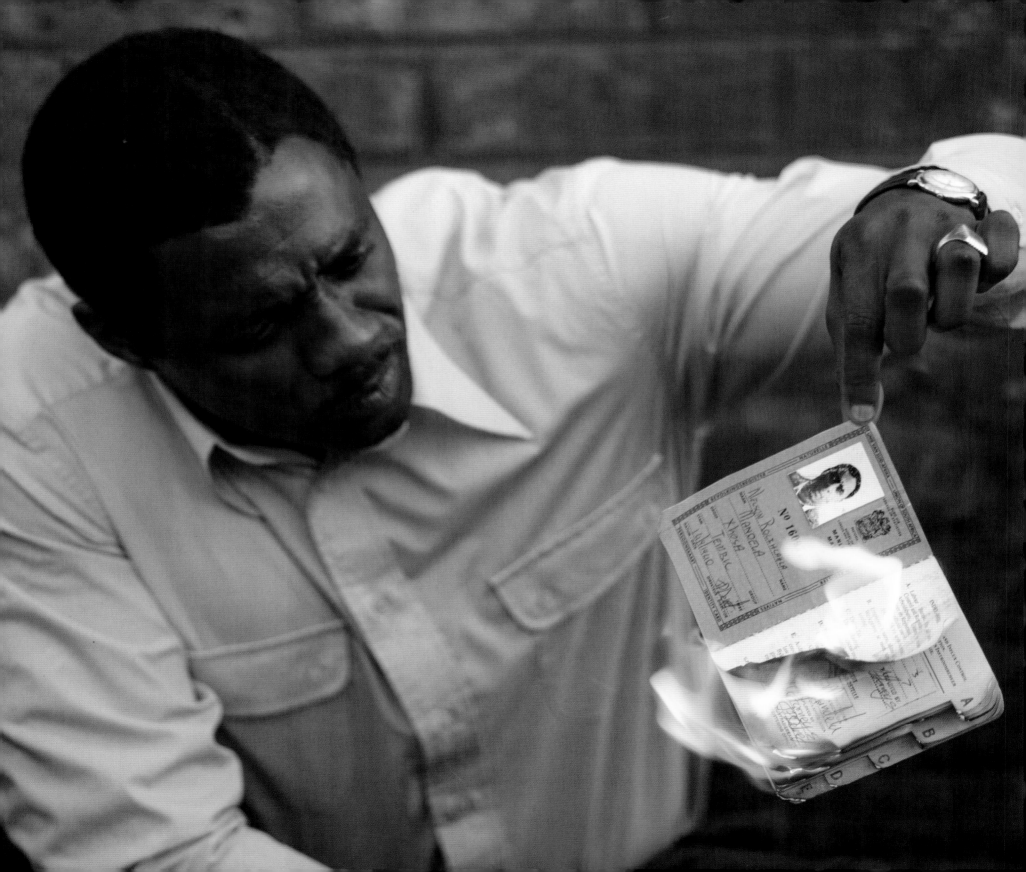

"WE NO LONGER ACCEPT THE AUTHORITY OF A STATE THAT MAKES WAR ON ITS PEOPLE."

The character Nelson Mandela, from the film *Mandela*

The massacre at Sharpeville created a new situation in the country. We in the ANC had to acknowledge the event in some way and give the people an outlet for their anger and grief. On March 26 a nationwide stay-at-home was announced as a national day of mourning and protest for the atrocities at Sharpeville. In Orlando I burned my pass before hundreds of people and dozens of press photographers.

Above left: A smiling Mandela about to burn his pass outside his Orlando home during the nationwide stay-at-home in March 1960. The stay-at-home led to the government declaring a state of emergency and arresting hundreds of activists, Mandela included.

Above right: Supporters threaten to burst through the gates outside the Drill Hall, Johannesburg, during the Treason Trial in which Mandela and 155 other activists were charged with high treason. The trial was an attempt by the government to suppress the power of the Congress Alliance who had orchestrated the adoption of a freedom charter at a mass rally in Kliptown, Soweto, in 1955. It lasted four and a half years, until all the charges were eventually withdrawn.

Left: Idris Elba, as Nelson Mandela, holds his burning pass.

"IT WAS FELT THAT SOMEBODY SHOULD GO UNDERGROUND AND LEAD THE MOVEMENT. I ACCEPTED THE CHALLENGE WITH ALL ITS DIFFICULTIES."

Nelson Mandela, from a BBC (UK) documentary, 1996

In 1961 it was decided that I would go underground. It was not a proposal that came as a surprise to me, nor was it one I particularly relished, but it was something I knew I had to do.

When I returned home from the meeting it was as though Winnie could read my thoughts. She knew I was about to embark on a life that neither of us wanted.

"Mandela is a proud man and not without a touch of vanity. By the time he went underground in 1961, his most recognizable feature was his beard. Photos of the bearded Mandela had appeared in newspapers and leaflets. An essential requirement [for his underground life] was that he be disguised and transformed into a 'new man.' He agreed to most suggestions but simply refused to shave. He must have known how the beard enhanced his looks and personality."

Ahmed Kathrada writes about Nelson Mandela going underground in the *Independent* (South Africa), July 11, 1998.

Above: Mandela's life on the run as South Africa's most wanted man led to the newspapers dubbing him the "Black Pimpernel."

Left: Idris Elba is seen portraying Nelson Mandela during the period he was underground.

"IT WAS ONLY WHEN ALL ELSE HAD FAILED, WHEN ALL CHANNELS OF PEACEFUL PROTEST HAD BEEN BARRED TO US, THAT THE DECISION WAS MADE TO EMBARK ON VIOLENT FORMS OF POLITICAL STRUGGLE, AND TO FORM UMKHONTO WE SIZWE."

Nelson Mandela, speech from the dock, Rivonia Trial, Palace of Justice, Pretoria, South Africa, April 20, 1964

In June 1961 the ANC authorized me to go ahead and form a new military organization, separate from the ANC. The policy of the ANC would still be that of nonviolence. The name of this new organization was Umkhonto we Sizwe (The Spear of the Nation)—or MK for short.

I immediately recruited Joe Slovo, and along with Walter Sisulu we formed the high command with myself as chairman. Through Joe, I enlisted the efforts of the white Communist Party members who had already executed acts of sabotage such as cutting government telephone and communication lines. Our mandate was to wage acts of violence against the state. Our intention was to begin with what was least violent to individuals but most damaging to the state.

Left: Liliesleaf Farm in the suburb of Rivonia was both a safe house during Mandela's underground years and the de facto headquarters of MK.

Far left: Members of MK watch on during a bomb-making demonstration in this image from the film.

Following page: Idris Elba, as Nelson Mandela, meets his family whilst in hiding in this scene at Liliesleaf Farm.

In October I moved to Liliesleaf Farm, located in Rivonia, a northern suburb of Johannesburg. I had taken the alias of David Motsamayi, and I wore the simple blue overalls that were the uniform of the black male servant. The loveliest times at the farm were when I was visited by Winnie and our daughters, Zenani and Zindzi. Winnie would visit me at the weekends. We were careful about her movements, and she would be picked up by one driver, dropped off at another place, and then picked up by a second driver before finally being delivered to the farm.

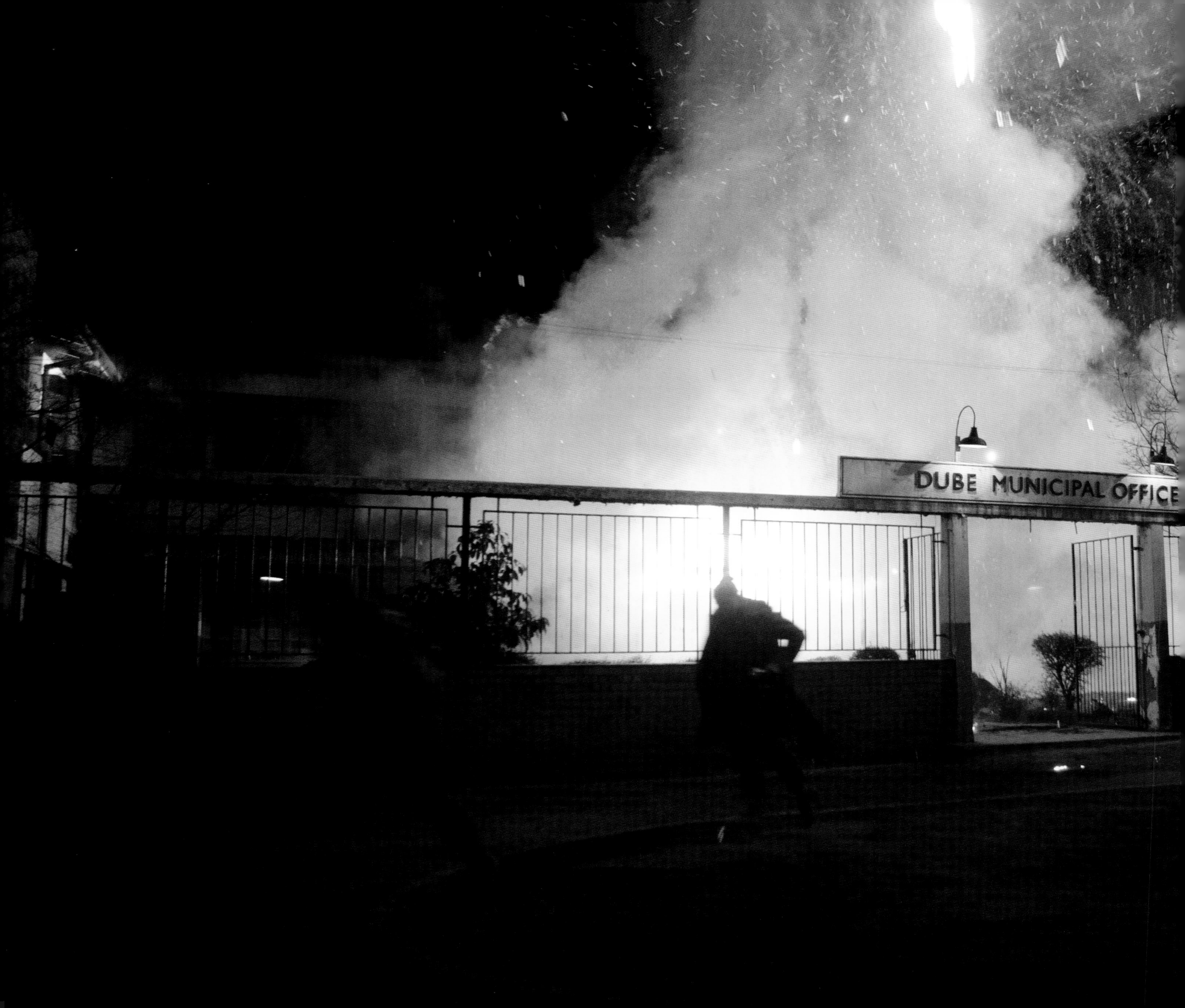
DUBE MUNICIPAL OFFICE

> "I DO NOT, HOWEVER, DENY THAT I PLANNED SABOTAGE. I DID NOT PLAN IT IN A SPIRIT OF RECKLESSNESS, NOR BECAUSE I HAVE ANY LOVE OF VIOLENCE. I PLANNED IT AS A RESU OF A CALM AND SOBER ASSESSMENT OF THE POLITICAL SITUATION THAT HAD ARISEN AFT MANY YEARS OF TYRANNY, EXPLOITATION, AN OPPRESSION OF MY PEOPLE BY THE WHITES."

Nelson Mandela, speech from the dock, Rivonia Trial, Palace of Justice, Pretoria, South Africa, April 20, 196

On the orders of the MK high command, in the early-morning hours of Decembe 16, 1961, homemade bombs were exploded at electric power stations and governmen offices in Johannesburg, Port Elizabeth, and Durban.

On the afternoon of July 11, 1963, a van drove up to the farm and dozens of arme policemen and several police dogs sprang out. They surrounded the property and entere the main building. The police confiscated hundreds of documents and papers, thoug they found no weapons. One of the most important documents was Operation Mayibuye a plan for guerilla warfare in South Africa. In one fell swoop, the police had captured th entire high command of Umkhonto we Sizwe.

Left: One of the original police photographs from the raid at Liliesleaf Farm on July 11, 1963, in which incriminating paperwork was found and almost the entire high command of MK was arrested.

Far left: A homemade bomb laid by members of MK explodes in the Dube Municipal Offices in this image from the film.

It was a cool, clear day and I reveled in the beauty of the Natal countryside as Cecil Williams and I passed through Howick, twenty miles northwest of Pietermaritzburg. At Cedara, a small town just past Howick, I noticed a Ford V8 filled with white men shoot past us on the right. I instinctively turned round to look behind and saw two more cars filled with white men. Suddenly, in front of us, the Ford was signaling to us to stop. I knew in that instant that my life on the run was over.

When our car stopped, a tall man came over to the window. He introduced himself as Sergeant Vorster of the Pietermaritzburg police and produced an arrest warrant. He asked me to identify myself. I told him my name was David Motsamayi. He nodded, and then asked me a few questions about where I had been and where I was going. Then he said, "Ag, you're Nelson Mandela, and this is Cecil Williams, and you are under arrest!"

above: The front page of the *Rand Daily Mail* proclaims that Mandela has finally been arrested after evading the authorities for two years. While he was underground he clandestinely exited South Africa, visiting twelve African states and receiving military training in Morocco and Ethiopia. He also visited London, UK. Following his arrest on August 5, 1962, he was charged with leaving the country without a passport and inciting workers to strike, and was sentenced to five years' imprisonment. He was incarcerated in Pretoria Central Prison and then on Robben Island. However, two weeks after his arrival on the island he was sent back to Pretoria, where, together with other members of MK's high command, he was charged with sabotage and faced the death penalty.

right: Idris Elba, in the character of Nelson Mandela, is arrested outside the white town of Howick.

"THE WORLD AROUND ME LITERALLY CRUMBLED..."

Nelson Mandela, from a letter to Zindzi Mandela about being arrested for treason in 1956, written on Robben Island, March 1, 1981

On October 9, 1963, we were driven to the Palace of Justice in Pretoria for the opening of "The State versus the National High Command and Others," better known as the Rivonia Trial. We were charged with sabotage and conspiracy.

The state case continued during the Christmas season of 1963, ending on February 29, 1964. For Rusty Bernstein, Raymond Mhlaba, and Ahmed Kathrada, the evidence of involvement in conspiracy was slight and we decided they should not incriminate themselves. The remaining six of us would make admissions of guilt on certain charges.

"In the weeks leading up to the sentence, Mandela never wavered. He knew what he was going to do. I think they all did. Once the decision had been taken that they were not going to deny the allegations, he started working on his statement from the dock.

"The decision to run a political defense, in essence to plead a justification, was undoubtedly correct. It had a huge impact internally and internationally. In fact, it put the government on the defensive; they were called upon to justify apartheid and they got lost attempting to do so. Yutar and his team were totally outclassed—the accused ran rings round them."

Arthur Chaskalson, one of the defense counsel in the Rivonia Trial, describes the accused's decision to admit all charges.

Above left: Crowds gather in front of the Palace of Justice in Pretoria in this image of the Rivonia Trial from the film.

Above right: Naomie Harris, playing Winnie Mandela, with Zikhona Sodlaka, as Nosekeni Fanny, Mandela's mother.

Far left: Winnie attends the Rivonia Trial with Mandela's mother, Nosekeni Fanny. Winnie had to fight a banning order to be allowed to attend.

"WHY IS IT THAT IN THIS COURTROOM I FACE A WHITE MAGISTRATE, AM CONFRONTED BY A WHITE PROSECUTOR, AND ESCORTED INTO THE DOCK BY A WHITE ORDERLY? CAN ANYONE HONESTLY AND SERIOUSLY SUGGEST THAT IN THIS TYPE OF ATMOSPHERE THE SCALES OF JUSTICE ARE EVENLY BALANCED?"

Nelson Mandela, from his application for the recusal of the magistrate Mr. W. A. van Helsdingen,
Old Synagogue, Pretoria, South Africa, October 22, 1962

"In Pretoria's Supreme Court, prisoners in custody enter up a steep staircase which emerges in the center. A few minutes before the judge entered, a signal was given for the prisoners to be brought in. The first prisoner was Nelson Mandela. As he climbed the staircase and his head and shoulders appeared above the level of the dock, there was a ripple of excitement among the public."

Joel Joffe, one of the defense counsel in the Rivonia Trial, describes Mandela arriving in court to give his statement of defense.

Left: An evocative photograph of the stairs that led the Rivonia trialists to the dock.

Right and pages 70, 72–73, and 74–75: Images of the Rivonia Trial were filmed in a recreated setting of the Palace of Justice.

"IT IS AN IDEAL WHICH I HOPE TO LIVE FOR AND TO ACHIEVE. BUT IF NEEDS BE, IT IS AN IDEAL FOR WHICH I AM PREPARED TO DIE."

Nelson Mandela, speech from the dock, Rivonia Trial, Palace of Justice, Pretoria, South Africa, April 20, 1964

I would be the first witness and therefore set the tone for the defense. We decided that instead of giving testimony, I would read a statement from the dock, while the others would testify and go through cross-examination.

On Monday, April 20, under the tightest of security, we were taken to the Palace of Justice, this time to begin our defense. Winnie was there with only my mother, and I nodded to them and we entered the court, which was again full. I rose and faced the courtroom and read slowly. After I had finished, the silence in the courtroom was complete. I had read for over four hours.

"It was our collective decision that Madiba should make the statement in the dock. We had seen Madiba's speech, we had discussed it, we agreed with it. We were aware that this speech could hang us, especially the last part of it. When we were discussing it, Madiba said, 'Apart from anything else, we owe it to the people in the struggle. If we show any weakness in our defense, or if we decide to appeal, it means we are showing weakness.'"

Ahmed Kathrada recalls the Rivonia trialists' decision that instead of being cross-examined, Mandela would make an unsworn statement of principle from the dock. Mandela, Kathrada, and five other trialists were flown directly to Robben Island the day after sentencing on June 12, 1964.

Above: Nelson Mandela's famous concluding paragraph in his statement from the dock at the Rivonia Trial.

Left: Idris Elba, as Nelson Mandela, delivers his speech from the dock in the Rivonia Trial.

"I THOUGHT OF THE LINE FROM SHAKESPEARE: 'BE ABSOLUTE FOR DEATH; FOR EITHER DEATH OR LIFE SHALL BE THE SWEETER.'"

Nelson Mandela, from *Long Walk to Freedom*, 1994

On June 11 we reassembled in the Palace of Justice for the verdict. We knew that for at least six of us there could be no verdict but guilty. The question was the sentence. Our judge in the Rivonia Trial, Mr. Quartus de Wet, announced each of the main accused guilty on all counts. That night, after a discussion among ourselves, Walter, Govan, and I informed counsel that whatever sentences we received, even the death sentence, we would not appeal. I was prepared for the death penalty.

① Statement from the dock

② If I meant everything I said

③ The blood of many patriots in this country have been shed for demanding treatment in conformity with civilised standards

④ That army is being grown

④ If I must die, let me declare for all to know that I will meet my fate like a man

Above: Mandela's notes to himself written while he and his fellow Rivonia trialists awaited sentencing. Should they have been sentenced to death, Mandela would have spoken from these notes on June 12. They read as follows: 1. Statement from the dock; 2. I meant everything I said; 3. The blood of many patriots in this country have [has] been shed for demanding treatment in conformity with civilized standards; 4. That army is beginning to grow; 4. [5.] If I must die, let me declare for all to know that I will meet my fate like a man.

Left: Idris Elba (Nelson Mandela), Zolani Mkiva (Raymond Mhlaba), Thapelo Mokoena (Elias Motsoaledi), Riaad Moosa (Ahmed Kathrada), Fana Mokoena (Govan Mbeki), Simo Magwaza (Andrew Mlangeni), and Tony Kgoroge (Walter Sisulu) deliberate over their fate in the holding cells of the Palace of Justice.

On Friday, June 12, 1964, we entered court for the last time. De Wet announce that he was not sentencing us to death, but life imprisonment. I turned and smile broadly to the gallery, searching out Winnie's face and that of my mother, but it w extremely confused in the court, with people shouting.

We were taken through the back of the building and entered a black van. To avoid th crowd, the van took a different route, but even so, we could hear the crowd shouti "*Amandla!*" and the slow, beautiful rhythms of "*Nkosi Sikelel' iAfrika.*"

"I WAS PREPARED FOR THE DEATH PENALTY. TO BE TRULY PREPARED FOR SOMETHING, ONE MUST ACTUALLY EXPECT IT. ONE CANNO BE PREPARED FOR SOMETHING WHILE SECRE BELIEVING IT WILL NOT HAPPEN. WE WERE A PREPARED, NOT BECAUSE WE WERE BRAVE B BECAUSE WE WERE REALISTIC."

Nelson Mandela, from *Long Walk to Freedom*, 1994

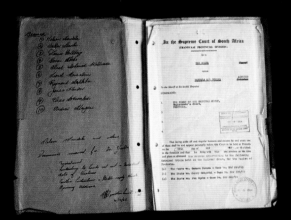

Above left: The front cover of the Rivonia Trial charge sheet listing the names of the accused.

Above right: The back page of the Rivonia Trial charge sheet listing the verdict against each of the accused

Left: The Rivonia Trialists rise to hear the verdict in this image from the film.

We landed at an airstrip on one end of the island. It was a grim, overcast day, and when I stepped out of the plane, the cold winter wind whipped through our thin prison uniforms. We were met by guards with automatic weapons; the atmosphere was tense. We were driven to the old jail, an isolated stone building, where we were ordered to strip while standing outside. When we were undressed, we were thrown the plain khaki uniforms of Robben Island.

"THIS IS THE ISLAND! YOU'LL NEVER LEAVE HERE AGAIN. YOU'LL NEVER TOUCH A WOMAN OR A CHILD AGAIN. THIS IS WHERE YOU DIE."

—The character Colonel Badenhorst, from the film *Mandela*

Right: The prisoners arrive on Robben Island to begin their life sentences. From left to right: Fana Mokoena as Govan Mbeki, Simo Magwaza as Andrew Mlangeni, Tony Kgoroge as Walter Sisulu, Idris Elba as Nelson Mandela, Riaad Moosa as Ahmed Kathrada, and Zolani Mkiva as Raymond Mhlaba.

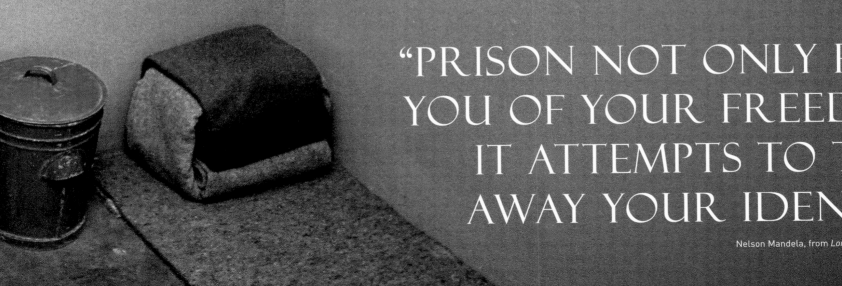

"PRISON NOT ONLY ROBS YOU OF YOUR FREEDOM, IT ATTEMPTS TO TAKE AWAY YOUR IDENTITY."

Nelson Mandela, from *Long Walk to Freedom*, 1994

That first week we began the work which would occupy us for the next few months. Each morning, a load of stones was dumped by the entrance to the courtyard. Using wheelbarrows, we moved the stones to the center of the yard. We were given either four-pound hammers, or fourteen-pound hammers for the larger stones. Our job was to crush the stones into gravel.

Within a few months our life had settled into a pattern. Prison life is about routine: each day like the one before; each week like the one before it, so that the months and years blend into each other.

The challenge for every prisoner, particularly every political prisoner, is how to survive prison intact, how to emerge from prison undiminished, how to conserve one's beliefs. I do not know how I could have done it if I had been alone. But the authority's greatest mistake was to keep us together, for together our determination was reinforced. We supported each other and gained strength from each other.

"The psychological pressures on us were immense. We'd be locked up twenty-three hours a day on weekends, half-an-hour exercise in the morning and half-an-hour in the afternoon, and if it was raining, we'd be locked up all day."

Prisoner Eddie Daniels describes conditions on Robben Island.

Far left: All day long the Robben Island prisoners sat in rows in the courtyard smashing stones into gravel.

Left: The watchtower and barbed-wire confines of Robben Island.

"PRISON—FAR FROM BREAKING OUR SPIRITS—MADE US MORE DETERMINED TO CONTINUE WITH THIS BATTLE UNTIL VICTORY WAS WON."

Nelson Mandela, from a conversation with Richard Stengel, March 10, 1993

One morning in early January, as we lined up to be counted before beginning work in the courtyard, we were instead marched outside and ordered into a covered truck. It was the first time that we had left our compound. A few minutes later we emerged from the truck in the lime quarry. It looked like an enormous white crater cut into the rocky hillside. After arriving in the morning, we would fetch our picks, shovels, hammers, and wheelbarrows from a zinc shed. Then we would assemble along the quarry face, usually in groups of three or four. Warders with automatic weapons stood on raised platforms watching us.

It was an attempt to crush our spirits. But those first few weeks in the quarry had the opposite effect on us. Despite blistered and bleeding hands, we were invigorated. I much preferred being outside, being able to see grass and trees, to observe birds flitting overhead, to feel the wind blowing in from the sea.

Above: In early 1965 the stone-breaking in the yard was replaced by a more grueling regime in a lime quarry where the blinding glare of the sun striking off the white stone seared the prisoners' eyes.

Right: Prisoners labor in the lime quarry—Idris Elba, playing Nelson Mandela, and the other black prisoners wear shorts, while Riaad Moosa, as Ahmed Kathrada, is seen in long pants. This was another way in which prison authorities reinforced the racial discrimination.

"On the night of sentence, the seven of us were woken up. I was chained to Govan Mbeki and put on the plane, past midnight, very cold, and we landed at Robben Island early on a cold, windy, and rainy Saturday morning. It was June 13, 1964. Now the first thing we had to do on Robben Island was change into prison clothes. In prison they had these gradations of apartheid—whites getting the best, then colored and Indians and Africans—so when it came to clothing, my colleagues, who were all older than me, had to wear short trousers with no socks, while I was given long trousers.

"So right through, our struggle was for equality, and after three years they conceded and equalized the clothing. As in most, if not all, improvements in prison, this came about as a result of a combination of pressures: pressure from the prisoners, from the struggle in the country, and from those in exile; and, as important, pressure from civil society organizations and individuals throughout the world."

Prisoner Ahmed Kathrada describes conditions on Robben Island.

"In the first years we had porridge without milk and very little sugar, and thin as water. You breakfasted at about six-thirty or seven and by about nine you were emptied, looking forward to lunch. Indians and colored prisoners would have mealie rice which used to be boiled at two or three in the morning, so by the time we had it at twelve we were eating rocks. And then, for good measure, a little bit of boiled pumpkin, turnip, carrots, just thrown on top, not necessarily all at once. You'd get pumpkin running for a year, two years, every lunch hour.

"The Africans had the same breakfast, but for lunch they'd have boiled mealies, yellow mealies. I liked something rough, so I used to exchange my food with an old man from the Transkei who was doing a life sentence for attempting to assassinate Matanzima. He had hardly any teeth so I used to exchange the samp or mealie rice for his mealies. For supper, Africans had more porridge and Indians and coloreds a quarter loaf of bread with a little bit of lard, and black coffee which was largely chicory. Four days a week you'd get beans, on the other days four little squares of meat."

Prisoner Billy Nair describes conditions on Robben Island.

Left: Prisoners are seen distributing meals to their fellow inmates in this image from the film.

Right: This photograph of Nelson Mandela mending his clothes in prison was taken by photographer Cloete Breytenbach circa 1964, and was staged by the authorities to create a false impression of the prisoners' lives. As soon as the press left, the prisoners returned to their task of smashing stones.

"WE SAW THAT NO PRISON WALLS OR GUARD DOGS OR EVEN THE COLD SEAS THAT ARE LIKE A DEADLY MOAT SURROUNDING ROBBEN ISLAND PRISON COULD EVER SUCCEED TO FRUSTRATE THE DESIRES OF ALL HUMANITY. WE DREW STRENGTH AND SUSTENANCE FROM THE KNOWLEDGE THAT WE WERE PART OF A GREATER HUMANITY THAN OUR JAILERS COULD CLAIM."

Nelson Mandela, from an address at the Cathedral of Uppsala, Uppsala, Sweden, March 13, 1990

"WHEN LETTERS DID ARRIVE, THEY WERE CHERISHED. A LETTER WAS LIKE THE SUMMER RAIN THAT COULD MAKE EVEN THE DESERT BLOOM."

Nelson Mandela, from *Long Walk to Freedom*, 1994

I was entitled to have only one visitor, and write and receive only one letter every six months. The island's censors would black out the offending passages in ink, but they later changed this when they realized we could wash away the ink and see what was underneath. They began to use razors to slice out whole paragraphs. Since most letters were written on both sides of the page, the material on the other side would also be excised. They seemed to relish delivering letters in tatters.

The anticipation of mail was overwhelming. Mail-call took place once a month, and sometimes six months would go by without a letter. When I was handed a letter by the authorities, I would not rush forward and grab it as I felt like doing, but take it in a leisurely manner. I would not give the authorities the satisfaction of seeing my eagerness. During the first few months, I received one letter from Winnie, but it was so heavily censored that not much more than the salutation was left.

Previous page, far left, and left:
As these images from the film portray, prison authorities exerted their power over the prisoners by various means such as humiliating body searches, and extreme censorship and control on distribution of private correspondence.

95

HYSICAL SUFFERING IS NOTHING COMPARED
O THE TRAMPLING DOWN OF THOSE TENDER
ONDS OF AFFECTION THAT FORM THE BASIS
F THE INSTITUTION OF MARRIAGE AND THE
AMILY THAT UNITE MAN AND WIFE. THIS IS
FRIGHTFUL MOMENT IN OUR LIFE."

lson Mandela, from a letter to Winnie Mandela, then in Pretoria Central Prison, written on Robben Island,
gust 1, 1970

At the end of August, after I had been on the island less than three months, I was
formed by the authorities that I would have a visitor the following day. I waited with
me anxiety, and suddenly on the other side of the window was Winnie's lovely face.
was tremendously frustrating not to be able to touch my wife, to speak tenderly to her,
have a private moment together.

could see immediately that Winnie was under tremendous strain. The banning and
rassment of my wife greatly troubled me; I could not look after her and the children,
d the state was making it difficult for her to look after herself. My powerlessness
awed at me.

the early hours of the morning of May 12, 1969, the security police woke Winnie at
r home and detained her without charge under the 1967 Terrorism Act, which gave the
vernment unprecedented powers of arrest and detention without trial. She was placed
solitary confinement in Pretoria, where she was denied bail and visitors; over the next
eks and months, she was relentlessly and brutally interrogated.

Left, right, following page left and right:
During Nelson Mandela's incarceration,
his wife Winnie also suffered from police
intimidation and underwent periods of
imprisonment herself. Naomie Harris,
playing Winnie Mandela, and Idris Elba,
as Nelson Mandela, are seen in their
respective prison cells.

"I FEEL AS IF I HAVE BEEN SOAKED IN GALL, EVERY PART OF ME, MY FLESH, BLOODSTREAM, BONE, AND SOUL, SO BITTER I AM

to be completely powerless to help you in the rough and fierce ordeals you are going through. What a world of difference to your failing health and to your spirit, darling, to my own anxiety and the strain that I cannot shake off, if only we could meet; if I could be on your side and squeeze you, or if I could but catch a glimpse of your outline through the thick wire netting that would inevitably separate us."

Nelson Mandela, from a letter to Winnie Mandela, then in Pretoria Central Prison, written on Robben Island, August 1, 1970

"MY DARLING,

. . . NOW AND AGAIN WE WILL VISIT THE FARM, WALK AROUND WITH FINGERS OF MY LEFT HAND DOVETAILING WITH THOSE OF YOUR RIGHT, WATCHING YOU DART OFF TO PLUCK SOME BEAUTIFUL WILD FLOWERS, JUST AS YOU DID ON SUNDAY, MARCH 10. YOU WERE DAZZLING IN THAT BLACK [AND] WHITE-SPOTTED NYLON DRESS. EVERY DAY WILL ALWAYS BE MARCH 10 FOR ME. WHAT DOES AGE AND LITTLE BLOOD PRESSURE MATTER TO US? NOTHING! . . . BUT YOU ARE A WITCH! ALWAYS CASTING SPELLS ON YOUR MAN . . ."

Nelson Mandela, from a letter to Winnie Mandela, written on Robben Island, December 28, 1970

My darlings,

Once again our beloved Mummy has been arrested and now she and Daddy are away in jail. My heart bleeds as I think of her sitting in some police station far away from home, perhaps alone and without anybody to talk to, and with nothing to read. Twenty-four hours of the day longing for her little ones. It may be many months or even years before you see her again. For long you may live like orphans without your own home and parents, without the natural love, affection and protection Mummy used to give you. Now you will get no birthday or Christmas parties, no presents or new dresses, no shoes or toys. Gone are the days when, after having a warm bath in the evening, you would sit at table with Mummy and enjoy her good and simple food. Gone are the comfortable beds, the warm blankets and clean linen she used to provide. She will not be there to arrange for friends to take you to bioscopes, concerts and plays, or to tell you nice stories in the evening, help you read difficult books and to answer the many questions you would like to ask. She will be unable to give you the help and guidance you need as you grow older and as new problems arise. Perhaps never again will Mummy and Daddy join you in House no. 8115 Orlando West, the one place in the whole world that is so dear to our hearts.

"ONCE AGAIN OUR BELOVED MUMMY HAS BEEN ARRESTED, AND NOW SHE AND DADDY ARE AWAY IN JAIL . . . FOR LONG YOU MAY LIVE LIKE ORPHANS WITHOUT YOUR OWN HOME AND PARENTS."

Nelson Mandela, from a letter to his daughters, Zenani and Zindzi Mandela, then aged nine and ten, written on Robben Island, June 23, 1969

Previous page: Winnie, played by Naomie Harris, walks through the South African veld in one of Mandela's drea

Left: In this image from the film, Zenani and Zindzi prepare breakfast for themselves in their mother's absenc

Time may seem to stand still for those of us in prison, but it did nothing for those outside. I was reminded of this when I was visited by my mother in spring 1968. Several weeks later, after returning from the quarry, I was told to go to head office to collect a telegram. It was from Makgatho, informing me that my mother had died of a heart attack. I immediately made a request to the commanding officer to be permitted to attend her funeral in the Transkei, which he turned down.

One cold morning in July 1969, I was called to the main office on Robben Island and handed a telegram. It was from my youngest son, Makgatho. He informed that my first and oldest son, Thembi, had been killed in a motor accident. What can one say about such a tragedy? I was already overwrought about my wife, I was still grieving for my mother, and then to hear such news. I do not have words to express the sorrow, or the loss I felt. It left a hole in my heart that can never be filled. I returned to my cell and lay on my bed. I do not know how long I stayed there, but I did not emerge for dinner. Some of the men looked in, but I said nothing. Finally, Walter came to me and knelt beside my bed, and I handed him the telegram. He said nothing, but only held my hand. I do not know how long he remained with me. There is nothing that one man can say to another at such a time.

Left: In 1969, Mandela's eldest son, twenty-four-year-old Thembi, was killed in a motor accident. Already distraught over Winnie's incarceration and still grieving the death of his mother, this tragedy left Mandela heartbroken.

Right: Idris Elba, as Nelson Mandela, requests permission to attend his son's funeral.

"SUDDENLY MY HEART SEEMED TO HAVE STOPPED BEATING AND THE WARM BLOOD THAT HAD FREELY FLOWN IN MY VEINS FOR THE LAST FIFTY-ONE YEARS FROZE INTO ICE. FOR SOME TIME I COULD NEITHER THINK NOR TALK AND MY STRENGTH APPEARED TO BE DRAINING OUT."

Nelson Mandela, from a letter to Irene Buthelezi, upon receiving the news of his son Thembi's death, written in Victor Verster Prison, Paarl, South Africa, August 3, 1969

On June 16, 1976, fifteen thousand schoolchildren gathered in Soweto to protest at the government's ruling that half of all classes in secondary schools must be taught in Afrikaans. A detachment of police confronted this army of earnest schoolchildren and without warning opened fire. Hundreds of children were wounded and killed.

The events of that day reverberated in every town and township of South Africa. The uprising triggered riots and violence across the country. Mass funerals for the victims of state violence became national rallying points. Suddenly the young people of South Africa were fired up with the spirit of protest and rebellion.

Above: In 1974 the government introduced the compulsory use of Afrikaans as the medium of instruction for pupils from Standard Five onwards. The rise of Black Consciousness in Soweto, spurred by the victory of the liberation movement Frelimo in Mozambique, lit a flame, and on June 16, 1976, thousands of youths marched through Soweto in protest. The police opened fire and a number of children were killed. Soweto became a battleground of stone-throwing youths against police with automatic rifles, tear gas, armored vehicles, and helicopters, and sparked a series of insurrections that lasted two years and spread throughout South Africa. Robben Island was swamped by a new breed of young activists as hundreds of youths were jailed. Others escaped to join the MK training camps abroad.

Previous page, following page, and pages 108–109: Idris Elba as Nelson Mandela in his cell on Robben Island.

Right: A recreation of the 1976 protests by school children following the introduction of Afrikaans as the language of instruction in black schools.

The oppression of my wife did not let up. In 1974 Winnie was charged with violating her banning orders, which restricted her from having any visitors apart from her children and her doctor. In 1976 I learned that Winnie had become involved with the Black Parents' Association, an organization of concerned local professionals and church leaders. The authorities seemed to be equally wary of the parents' association and the young rebels, and Winnie was detained under the Internal Security Act and imprisoned without charge for five months. She emerged from jail even firmer in her commitment to the struggle, and the authorities were dismayed about her popularity with the young radicals of Soweto.

On the night of May 16, 1977, police cars and a truck pulled up outside our house in Orlando West and began loading furniture and clothing into the back of the truck. This time Winnie was not being arrested, detained, or interrogated. She was being banished. In Brandfort she and Zindzi would be alone.

"THERE WERE MANY DARK MOMENTS WHEN MY FAITH IN HUMANITY WAS SORELY TEST- ED, BUT I WOULD NOT AND COULD NOT GIVE MYSELF UP TO DESPAIR. THAT WAY LAY DEFEAT AND DEATH."

Nelson Mandela, from *Long Walk to Freedom*, 1994

"EVERY DAY WE HEARD YOUR VOICES RING—'FREE THE POLITICAL PRISONERS!' WE HEARD YOUR VOICES SING—'LET MY PEOPLE GO!' AS WE HEARD THAT VIBRANT AND INVIGORATING CRY OF HUMAN CONCERN, WE KNEW THAT WE WOULD BE FREE."

Nelson Mandela, from an address at the Cathedral of Uppsala, Uppsala, Sweden, March 13, 1990

In September 1976, the isolation section was filled with young men who had been arrested in the aftermath of the Soweto uprising. These young men were a different breed of prisoner from those we had seen before. They were brave, hostile, and aggressive; they would not take orders, and shouted "*Amandla!*" at every opportunity.

Yet as we entered the new decade my hopes for South Africa rose once again. Some mornings I walked out into the courtyard and every living thing there, the seagulls and wagtails, the small trees, and even the stray blades of grass seemed to smile and shine in the sun. It was at such times, when I perceived the beauty of even this small, closed-in corner of the world, that I knew that someday my people and I would be free.

In the *Johannesburg Sunday Post* in March 1980, the headline was "FREE MANDELA!" Inside was a petition that people could sign to ask for my release and that of my fellow political prisoners. While newspapers were still barred from printing my picture or any words I had ever said or written, the *Post's* campaign ignited a public discussion of our release.

Above: Posters from both the Free Mandela and the British Anti-Apartheid Movement's campaigns. In the early 1980s Oliver Tambo, who was working for the ANC in exile in London, launched an anti-apartheid campaign to release all political prisoners. Mandela, now the most famous political prisoner in the world, was its figurehead. The Free Mandela campaign was subsequently launched by South Africa's *Sunday Post*, with the newspaper's petition for his release collecting eighty-six thousand signatures.

Left: Labour politician and chair of the British Anti-Apartheid Movement Bob Hughes (far right) and others march through London on an anti-apartheid march.

"OURS IS NOT TO ASK FOR EQUALITY ON A LOWER SCALE; OURS IS TO FIGHT TO WIN ON AN EQUAL BUT HIGHER LEVEL."

Prisoner Ahmed Kathrada describes Nelson Mandela's reaction to discrimination on Robben Island

On March 31, 1982, I was visited in my cell by the commanding officer and a number of prison officials. This was highly unusual; the CO did not generally pay calls on prisoners in their cells.

"Mandela," he said, "I want you to pack your things."

I asked him why.

"We are transferring you," he said simply.

"Where?"

"I cannot say," he replied.

The commanding officer left and went in turn to the cells of Walter, Raymond Mhlaba, and Andrew Mlangeni and gave them the same order. Within minutes we were on board the ferry headed for Cape Town. At the docks we were hustled into a windowless truck. The four of us stood in the dark while the truck drove for what seemed considerably more than an hour. We passed through various checkpoints, and finally came to a stop. The back doors swung open, and in the dark we were marched up some concrete steps and through metal doors into another security facility. I managed to ask a guard where we were.

"Pollsmoor Prison," he said.

Above: Nelson Mandela and his fellow prisoners are transferred from Robben Island to Pollsmoor Prison on the mainland.

Right: From left to right: Idris Elba as Nelson Mandela, Simo Magwaza as Andrew Mlangeni, Zolani Mkhiva as Raymond Mhlaba, and Riaad Moosa as Ahmed Kathrada.

Pollsmoor Maximum Security Prison is on the edge of a prosperous white suburb called Tokai, a few miles southeast of Cape Town. There were four beds, with sheets, and towels, a great luxury for men who had spent much of the last eighteen years sleeping on thin mats on a stone floor. Compared with Robben Island, we were in a five-star hotel.

In May 1984, on a scheduled visit from Winnie, Zenani, and her youngest daughter, I was escorted into a separate room where there was only a small table, and no dividers of any kind. That day was the beginning of what were known as "contact" visits. Before either of us knew it, we were in the same room in each other's arms. I kissed and held my wife for the first time in all these many years. It was a moment I had dreamed about a thousand times. I held her to me for what seemed like an eternity. We were all still and silent except for the sound of our hearts. I did not want to let go of her at all, but I broke free and embraced my daughter and then I took her child onto my lap.

"IT HAD BEEN TWENTY-ONE YEARS SINCE I HAD EVEN TOUCHED MY WIFE'S HAND."

Nelson Mandela, from *Long Walk to Freedom*, 1994

Left: Idris Elba and Naomie Harris portray Nelson and Winnie's first embrace in twenty-one years, in the prison visiting room.

"YOUR FREEDOM
AND MINE CANNOT BE
SEPARATED. I WILL RETURN."

Nelson Mandela, from Pollsmoor Prison, Cape Town, South Africa, February 10, 1985

Above left: In front of a packed Jabulani stadium in Soweto, Zindzi Mandela reads a speech on behalf of her father in response to P. W. Botha's offer of conditional release, February 1985.

Left and above right: Lindiwe Matshikiza, playing Zindzi Mandela, reads Mandela's response to the offer of conditional release in front of crowds of supporters.

At Pollsmoor, we were more connected to outside events. We were aware that the struggle was intensifying and had captured the attention of the world.

Faced with trouble at home and pressure from abroad, P. W. Botha offered a tepid, halfway measure. On January 31, 1985, the state president publicly offered me my freedom if I "unconditionally rejected violence as a political instrument." I wrote to the foreign minister rejecting the conditions for my release. I wanted to reassure the ANC that my loyalty to the organization was beyond question and to send a message to the government that while I rejected its offer because of the conditions attached to it, I nevertheless thought negotiation, not war, was the path to a solution.

I met Winnie and gave her the speech I had prepared. On Sunday, February 10, 1985, my daughter Zindzi read my response to a cheering crowd of people who had not been able to hear my words legally anywhere in South Africa for more than twenty years.

In 1985 I was taken to a new cell away from my friends, three floors below and in an entirely different wing. I was not happy to be separated from my colleagues, but my solitude gave me a certain liberty, and I resolved to use it to do something I had been pondering for a long while: begin discussions with the government. I chose to tell no one what I was about to do.

In 1987 I had several private meetings with Kobie Coetsee, the minister of justice, at his residence, and later that year the government appointed a committee of senior officials to conduct private discussions with me.

I requested to see my colleagues. I would seek their counsel about the idea of having talks with the government without mentioning that an actual committee had been formed. Sisulu and Kathy's response was negative; they were resolutely against what I was suggesting. Raymond and Andrew were in favor.

"WE KNOW THAT ONE DAY WE'LL BE FREE.

We'll be rulers of our country. Do we want to fall into the same hell that you lie in now? Do we want to hate you, and hurt you, and fear you, and know it can never end? That would be to lock ourselves in prison all over again. And our children. And our children's children. So I tell you, gentlemen, we have no choice. When we come to power, there will be no revenge."

The character Nelson Mandela, from the film *Mandela*

Left: Idris Elba (Nelson Mandela) meets with members of the white-minority government, Deon Lotz (Kobie Coetsee), Andre Stoltz (General Willemse), A. J. van de Merwe (Fanie van der Merwe), and Carl Beukes (Niel Barnard).

I was told in the winter of 1988 that President Botha was planning to see me before the end of August. The country was in upheaval and the townships were on the brink of open warfare. The government had reimposed a state of emergency in both 1987 and 1988. International pressure mounted. More companies left South Africa. The American Congress had passed a sweeping sanctions bill.

In the mid-1980s, violence in the country escalated alarmingly and a state of emergency was declared. **Above, clockwise from top left:** Vigilantes at a squatter camp; police charge United Democratic Front supporters marching for the release of political prisoners en route to Pollsmoor Prison in 1985; residents flee the violence in the squatter camps; mourners are tear-gassed at a 1986 funeral.

Left and following page: Protests and violent altercations increased during the late 1980s, as seen in these images from the film.

"I KNEW AS WELL AS I KNEW ANYTHING THAT THE OPPRESSOR MUST BE LIBERATED JUST AS SURELY AS THE OPPRESSED. A MAN WHO TAK AWAY ANOTHER MAN'S FREEDOM IS A PRISON OF HATRED; HE IS LOCKED BEHIND THE BARS OF PREJUDICE AND NARROW-MINDEDNESS. I AM NOT TRULY FREE IF I AM TAKING AWAY SOMEONE ELSE'S FREEDOM, JUST AS SURE AS I AM NOT FREE WHEN MY HUMANITY IS TAKE FROM ME. THE OPPRESSED AND THE OPPRESS ALIKE ARE ROBBED OF THEIR HUMANITY."

Nelson Mandela, from *Long Walk to Freedom*, 1994

Above: A woman escapes a squatter camp in the Cape with a piece of corrugated iron, all that is left of her house after battles between vigilantes.

"WE SHALL NEVER FORGET
HOW MILLIONS OF PEOPLE
AROUND THE WORLD
JOINED US IN SOLIDARITY
TO FIGHT THE INJUSTICE OF
OUR OPPRESSION WHILE
WE WERE INCARCERATED."

Nelson Mandela speaking at a Live 8 concert, Mary Fitzgerald Square, Johannesburg, South Africa, July 2, 2005

Right: A pop concert in London's Wembley Stadium to celebrate Mandela's seventieth birthday was broadcast around the world, July 1988.

"I HAVE OFTEN WONDERED WHETHER A PERSON IS JUSTIFIED IN NEGLECTING HIS OWN FAMILY TO FIGHT FOR OPPORTUNITIES FOR OTHERS."

Nelson Mandela, from an unpublished autobiographical manuscript, written on Robben Island, 1975

On the evening of December 9, 1988, Major Marais came into my room and told me to prepare to leave. "Where to?" I asked him. He could not say. We left in a rush, and after about an hour on the road we entered a prison whose name I recognized: Victor Verster. Located in the lovely old Cape Dutch town of Paarl, Victor Verster is thirty-five miles northeast of Cape Town. We drove along a winding dirt road through a wooded area at the rear of the property. At the end of the road we came to an isolated whitewashed one-story cottage set behind a concrete wall and shaded by tall fir trees.

That July, for my seventy-first birthday, I was visited at the cottage at Victor Verster by nearly my entire family. It was the first time I had ever had my wife and children and grandchildren all in one place, and it was a grand and very happy occasion.

Right: Idris Elba, as Nelson Mandela, is surrounded by his family on the day of his release.

130

"YOUR PEOPLE HAVE TAKEN FROM ME HALF MY LIFE. NOW YOU RETURN ME, AN OLD MAN, TO A FAMILY THAT HAS GROWN UP WITHOUT ME, TO A HOME THAT HAS BEEN LONG ABANDONED. I DON'T WANT YOU BY MY SIDE IN THAT MOMENT. I DON'T WANT TO BE TOLD THAT YOU HAVE GIVEN ME MY FREEDOM. JUST OPEN THE GATES, AND LET ME GO."

The character Nelson Mandela, from the film *Mandela*

On October 10, 1989, President de Klerk announced that Walter Sisulu and seven of my former Robben Island comrades were to be released.

In early December I was informed that a meeting with de Klerk was set for the twelfth of that month. I then drafted a letter to de Klerk. The subject was talks between the government and the ANC. On the morning of December 13 I was taken to Tuynhuys. From the first I noticed that Mr. de Klerk listened to what I had to say. This was a novel experience. National Party leaders generally heard what they wanted to hear in discussions with black leaders, but Mr. de Klerk seemed to be making a real attempt to listen and understand.

On February 2, 1990, F. W. de Klerk stood before Parliament to make the traditional opening speech and did something no other South African head of state had ever done: he truly began to dismantle the apartheid system and lay the groundwork for a democratic South Africa.

Left: Idris Elba, playing Nelson Mandela, and Gys de Villiers, as President de Klerk, begin negotiations between the government and the ANC.

"AS I FINALLY WALKED THROUGH THOSE GATES I FELT—EVEN AT THE AGE OF SEVENTY-ONE—THAT MY LIFE WAS BEGINNING ANEW. MY TEN THOUSAND DAYS OF IMPRISONMENT WERE AT LAST OVER."

Nelson Mandela, from *Long Walk to Freedom*, 1994

I awoke on the day of my release after only a few hours' sleep. There were already dozens of people at the house, and the scene took on the aspect of a celebration.

At first I could not really make out what was going on, but when I was within 150 feet or so, I saw a great crowd of people: hundreds of photographers and television cameras and newspeople as well as several thousand well-wishers. I was astounded and a little alarmed. When I was among the crowd I raised my right fist, and there was a roar. I had not been able to do that for twenty-seven years and it gave me a surge of strength and joy.

Above: On February 11, 1990, nine days after President F. W. de Klerk had announced the unbanning of the ANC and other banned liberation organizations, Mandela was released. With Winnie by his side he walked through the gates of Victor Verster Prison and raised his fist in the ANC salute.

Right: Idris Elba and Naomie Harris re-enact the release of Nelson Mandela from Victor Verster Prison.

"FRIENDS, COMRADES, AND FELLOW SOUTH AFRICANS. I GREET YOU ALL IN THE NAME OF PEACE, DEMOCRACY, AND FREEDOM FOR ALL. I STAND HERE BEFORE YOU NOT AS A PROPHET BUT AS A HUMBLE SERVANT OF YOU, THE PEOPLE. YOUR TIRELESS AND HEROIC SACRIFICES HAVE MADE IT POSSIBLE FOR ME TO BE HERE TODAY. I THEREFORE PLACE THE REMAINING YEARS OF MY LIFE IN YOUR HANDS."

Nelson Mandela, from the first speech after his release, City Hall, Cape Town, South Africa, February 11, 1990

"After sentencing in the Rivonia Trial, we were taken back to the prison in an armored convoy with the sirens shrieking, and when we arrived, Colonel Aucamp, the head of prison security, said to me, 'You're lucky. You should have been hanged, all of you. You will never get out of here on your own feet. We will carry you out in a box.' He was smiling like a cat that had licked the cream. At the time I was amazed at the viciousness of his response; they really were bitter that we got away with our lives. But whether or not he had heard Colonel Aucamp that day, when Nelson Mandela was released, he stopped the car inside the prison grounds and he walked out. And it seemed to me a moment of such triumph, that this man, dressed in a suit, elegant as ever, should walk out on his own feet to meet the crowds."

Denis Goldberg, co-defendant in the Rivonia Trial and the only white man among those of the accused to be found guilty, describes the moment Mandela walked to freedom.

Left: Mandela addresses the people from the balcony of Cape Town City Hall on his release from prison, February 11, 1990. Flanking him are Walter Sisulu to his right and Cyril Ramaphosa.

In July 1991 the ANC held its first annual conference inside South Africa in thirty years. At the conference I was elected president of the ANC without opposition. On December 20, 1991, after more than a year and a half of talks about talks, the real talks began: CODESA—the Convention for a Democratic South Africa—represented the first formal negotiations forum between the government, the ANC, and other South African parties.

Of all the issues that hindered the peace process, none was more devastating and frustrating than the escalation of violence in the country. We had all hoped that as negotiations got under way, violence would decrease. But, in fact, the opposite happened. The police and security forces were making very few arrests. People in the townships were accusing them of aiding and abetting the violence.

On the night of June 17, 1992, a heavily armed force of Inkatha Freedom Party members secretly raided the Vaal township of Boipatong and killed forty-six people.

Left: Street fighting between Inkatha Freedom Party and ANC supporters.

Following page: Idris Elba, as Nelson Mandela, comforts a mourner in the aftermath of the Boipatong massacre.

Someone gave me this note here, when I was leaving Boipatong. I want to read it to you. It says, 'No peace. Do not talk about peace. We've had enough. Please, Mr. Mandela, no peace. Give us weapons. No peace.' Here's my answer. There is only one way forward— and that is peace. I have given my life to this struggle. I have been willing to die. I have lost twenty-seven years of my life in prison. But I say to you now, I forgive them.

IF I CAN FORGIVE THEM—SO CAN YOU."

The character Nelson Mandela, from the film *Mandela*

Four days after the murders, I publicly warned de Klerk that if he sought to impose new measures to restrict demonstrations or free expression, the ANC would launch a nationwide defiance campaign with myself as the first volunteer.

Although few people will remember June 3, 1993, it was a landmark in South African history. On that day, after months of negotiations at the World Trade Center, the multiparty forum voted to set a date for the country's first national, nonracial, one-person–one-vote election: April 27, 1994. For the first time in South African history, the black majority would go to the polls to elect their own leaders.

Right: Winnie Mandela, played by Naomie Harris, addresses a crowd in a scene from the film.

Left: As tension increases, Idris Elba, as Nelson Mandela, calls on his fellow South Africans to renounce violence and move towards a peaceful and democratic nation.

On April 13, 1992, at a press conference in Johannesburg, flanked by my two oldest friends and comrades, Walter and Oliver, I announced my separation from my wife. The situation had grown so difficult that I felt it was in the best interests of all concerned—the ANC, the family, and Winnie—that we part. Although I discussed the matter with the ANC, the separation itself was made for personal reasons.

"I PART FROM MY WIFE WITH NO RECRIMINATIONS. I EMBRACE HER WITH ALL THE LOVE AND AFFECTION I HAVE NURSED FOR HER INSIDE AND OUTSIDE PRISON FROM THE MOMENT I FIRST MET HER."

Nelson Mandela, announcing his separation from Winnie Mandela, Johannesburg, South Africa, April 13, 1992

Left: Idris Elba is seen playing Nelson Mandela as he moves to his own residence following his separation from Winnie.

The images of South Africans going to the polls that day are burned in my memory. Great lines of patient people snaking through the dirt roads and streets of towns and cities; old women who had waited half a century to cast their first vote saying that they felt like human beings for the first time in their lives; white men and women saying they were proud to live in a free country at last. The violence and bombings ceased, and it was as though we were a nation reborn.

I marked an X in the box next to the letters ANC and then slipped my folded ballot paper into a simple wooden box. I had cast the first vote of my life.

"The moment for which I had waited so long came and I folded my ballot paper and cast my vote. Wow! I shouted, 'Yippee!' It was giddy stuff. It was like falling in love. The sky looked blue and more beautiful. I saw the people in a new light. They were beautiful, they were transfigured. I, too, was transfigured. It was dream-like."

Archbishop Desmond Tutu describes voting for the first time.

Above: Whites and blacks queue for hours to cast their vote on April 27, 1994, in South Africa's first democratic elections.

Left: Jubilant black South Africans wait patiently in line to vote for the first time in this scene from the film.

Following page: Idris Elba, playing Nelson Mandela, celebrates with supporters at the ANC victory party.

"IT IS THE REALIZATION OF HOPES AND DREAMS THAT WE HAVE CHERISHED OVER DECADES."

Nelson Mandela, after voting for the first time, Ohlange High School, South Africa, April 27, 1994

On the day of the inauguration, May 10, 1994, I was overwhelmed with a sense of history. In the first decade of the twentieth century, the white-skinned peoples of South Africa patched up their differences and erected a system of racial domination against dark-skinned peoples of their own land. The structure they created formed the basis of one of the harshest, most inhumane societies the world has ever known. Now, in the last decade of the twentieth century, and my own eighth decade as a man, that system had been overturned forever and replaced by one that recognized the rights and freedoms of all peoples, regardless of the color of their skin.

On the podium, Mr. de Klerk was first sworn in as second deputy president. Then Thabo Mbeki was sworn in as first deputy president. When it was my turn, I pledged to obey and uphold the constitution and to devote myself to the well-being of the republic and its people.

Above: The "rainbow nation" celebrates the birth of South Africa's Government of National Unity. In the election, the ANC won 62.6 percent of the vote and 252 of the 400 seats in the new Parliament.

Right: Mandela and his daughter Zenani at Mandela's inauguration as President of South Africa on May 10, 1994.

"NEVER, NEVER, AND NEVER AGAIN SHALL IT BE THAT THIS BEAUTIFUL LAND WILL AGAIN EXPERIENCE THE OPPRESSION OF ONE BY ANOTHER . . . THE SUN SHALL NEVER SET ON SO GLORIOUS A HUMAN ACHIEVEMENT. LET FREEDOM REIGN."

Nelson Mandela, from an address on his inauguration as President of South Africa, Union Buildings, Pretoria, South Africa, May 10, 1994

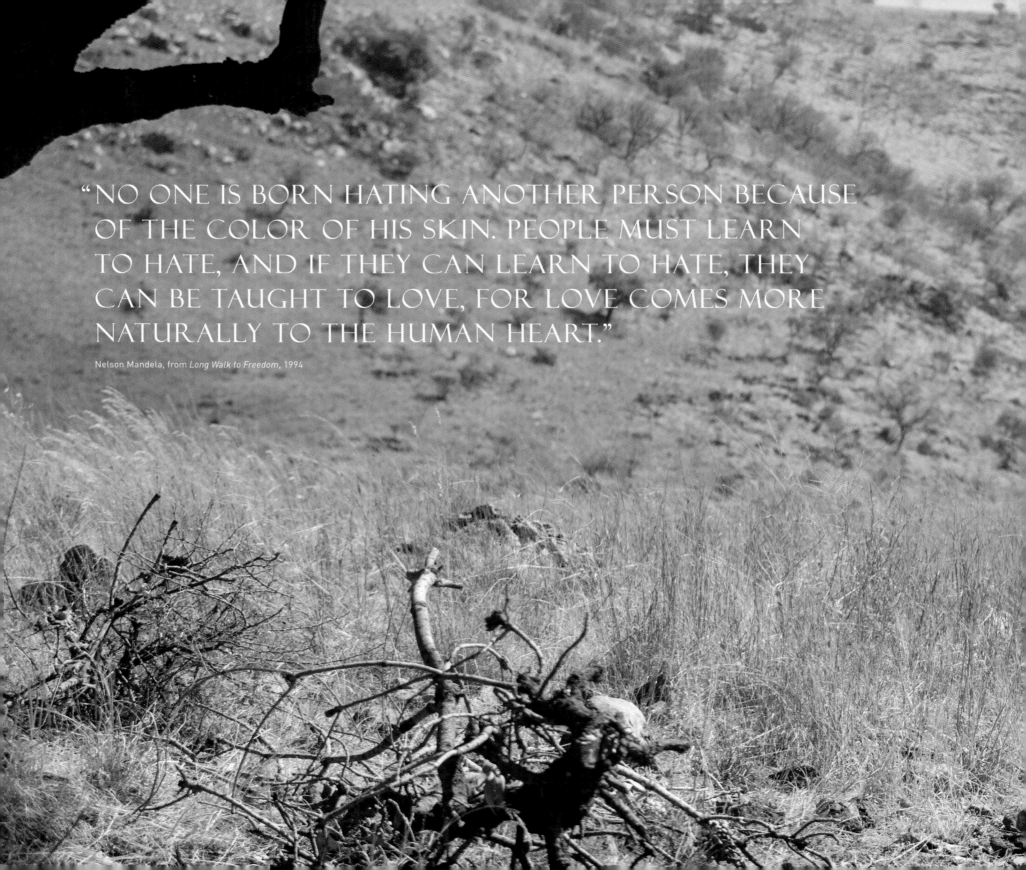

"NO ONE IS BORN HATING ANOTHER PERSON BECAUSE OF THE COLOR OF HIS SKIN. PEOPLE MUST LEARN TO HATE, AND IF THEY CAN LEARN TO HATE, THEY CAN BE TAUGHT TO LOVE, FOR LOVE COMES MORE NATURALLY TO THE HUMAN HEART."

Nelson Mandela, from *Long Walk to Freedom*, 1994

NELSON MANE

1918: Rolihlahla Mandela is born on July 18, at Mvezo in the Transkei, to Nosekeni Fanny and Nkosi Mphakanyiswa Gadla Mandela.

1925: Attends primary school near the village of Qunu. His teacher gives him the name Nelson.

1930: Following the death of his father, Mandela is entrusted to the care of Chief Jongintaba Dalindyebo, the regent of the Thembu people. He goes to live with him in Mqhekezweni at the Great Place.

1934: Undergoes the traditional circumcision ritual, initiating him into manhood. He attends Clarkebury Boarding Institute in Engcobo.

1937: Attends Healdtown, a Wesleyan College in Fort Beaufort.

1939: Enrolls at the University College of Fort Hare, Alice, the only black university in South Africa. Meets Oliver Tambo.

1940: Expelled from Fort Hare for embarking on protest action.

1941: Escapes an arranged marriage and moves to Johannesburg where he finds work in the gold mines as a night watchman. Meets Walter Sisulu, who finds him employment as an articled clerk at the law firm Witkin, Sidelsky, and Eidelman.

1942: Continues studying for his bachelor of arts degree (BA) by correspondence through the University of South Africa (UNISA). Begins to attend African National Congress (ANC) meetings informally.

1943: Graduates with a BA and enrolls for a bachelor of laws degree (LLB) at the University of the Witwatersrand.

1944: Co-founds the ANC Youth League (ANCYL). Marries Evelyn Ntoko Mase and they have four children: Thembekile (1945–69); Makaziwe (1947), who died at nine months old; Makgatho (1950–2005); and Makaziwe (1954–).

1948: Elected national secretary of the ANCYL, and onto the Transvaal National Executive of the ANC.

1951: Elected president of the ANCYL.

1952: Elected ANC president of the Transvaal province and is automatically a deputy president of the ANC. Public spokesperson and national volunteer-in-chief of the Defiance Campaign, which begins on June 26, 1952. He is arrested on a number of occasions and spends several days in jail. He is convicted with nineteen others under the Suppression of Communism Act and sentenced to nine months'

imprisonment with hard labor, suspended for two years, and also receives the first in a series of banning orders preventing him from participating in any political activity. With Oliver Tambo he opens Mandela and Tambo, South Africa's first African law partnership.

1953: Devises the M-Plan for the ANC's future underground operations.

1955: The Freedom Charter is adopted at the Congress of the People in Kliptown. Mandela, along with other banned comrades, watches the proceedings in secret, from the roof of a nearby shop.

1956: Arrested and charged with treason along with 155 members of the Congress Alliance. The trial continues for four and a half years.

1958: Divorces Evelyn Mase. Marries Nomzamo Winifred Madikizela and they have two daughters: Zenani (1959–) and Zindziswa (1960–).

1960: Following the Sharpeville Massacre on March 21, the government declares a state of emergency and Mandela is detained. On April 8, the ANC and PAC (Pan Africanist Congress) are banned.

1961: Acquitted in the last group of twenty-eight in the 1956 Treason Trial; all the other accused had charges withdrawn at different stages of the trial. In March, Mandela appears at the All-in African Conference in Pietermaritzburg as the main speaker and demands a national convention to draw up a new constitution for South Africa. In April, he goes underground. In June, the armed wing of the ANC, Umkhonto we Sizwe (MK), is formed with Mandela as its first commander-in-chief, and launched on December 16 with a series of explosions.

1962: In January, Mandela departs South Africa to undergo military training and to garner support for the ANC. He leaves the country clandestinely through Botswana (then Bechuanaland) and re-enters South Africa from there in July. He receives military training in Ethiopia and in Morocco, close to the border of Algeria. In total he visits twelve African states, and also spends two weeks in London, UK, with Oliver Tambo. On August 5 he is arrested near Howick in KwaZulu-Natal, and is sentenced to five years' imprisonment on November 7 for leaving the country without a passport and inciting workers to strike.

1963: Mandela is transferred to Robben Island Prison on May 27, before being suddenly returned to Pretoria Central Prison two weeks later. On July 11, police raid Liliesleaf

Farm in Rivonia and arrest almost all of the high command of MK. In October, Mandela is put on trial for sabotage with nine others in what becomes known as the Rivonia Trial.

1964: In March, James Kantor has charges withdrawn. In June, Rusty Bernstein is acquitted, but Mandela, Walter Sisulu, Ahmed Kathrada, Govan Mbeki, Raymond Mhlaba, Denis Goldberg, Andrew Mlangeni, and Elias Motsoaledi are convicted and sentenced to life imprisonment. All except Goldberg, who serves his sentence in Pretoria, are taken to Robben Island Prison.

1968: Mandela's mother dies on September 26. His request to attend her funeral is refused.

1969: Mandela's eldest son, Madiba Thembekile (Thembi), is killed in a car accident on July 13. Mandela's letter to the prison authorities requesting permission to attend his funeral is ignored.

1975: Begins writing his autobiography in secret. Sisulu and Kathrada review the manuscript and make comments. Mac Maharaj and Laloo Chiba transcribe it into tiny handwriting, and Chiba conceals it inside Maharaj's exercise books. It is smuggled out by Maharaj when he is released in 1976.

1982: Mandela along with Walter Sisulu, Raymond Mhlaba, Andrew Mlangeni, and, later, Ahmed Kathrada are sent to Pollsmoor Prison. They share a large communal cell on the top floor of a cell block.

1984: Rejects an offer by his nephew K. D. Matanzima, the president of the so-called independent state (or bantustan) of Transkei, to be released into the Transkei.

1985: Rejects President P. W. Botha's offer to release him if he renounces violence as a political strategy. On February 10 his statement of rejection is read out to a rally in Soweto by his daughter Zindzi. In November, Mandela undergoes prostate surgery in the Volks Hospital. He is visited in hospital by the minister of justice, Kobie Coetsee. On his return to prison, he is held alone. Begins exploratory talks with members of the government over the creation of conditions for negotiations with the ANC.

1988: A twelve-hour pop concert to celebrate Mandela's seventieth birthday, held at Wembley Stadium, London, UK, is broadcast to sixty-seven countries. Contracts tuberculosis and is admitted to Tygerberg Hospital, then Constantiaberg Medi-Clinic. He is discharged in December and moved to Victor Verster Prison, near Paarl.

1989: Graduates with an LLB degree through the University of South Africa.

1990: The ANC is unbanned on February 2. Mandela is released from prison on February 11.

1991: Elected ANC president at the first ANC national conference in South Africa since its banning in 1960.

1993: Awarded the Nobel Peace Prize with President F. W. de Klerk.

1994: Votes for the first time in his life in South Africa's first democratic elections on April 27. On May 9, he is elected first president of a democratic South Africa and, on May 10, he is inaugurated as president in Pretoria. His autobiography, *Long Walk to Freedom*, is published.

1996: Divorces Winnie Mandela.

1998: Marries Graça Machel on his eightieth birthday.

1999: Steps down after one term as president.

2001: Diagnosed with prostate cancer.

2004: Announces he is stepping down from public life.

2005: Makgatho, Mandela's second-born son, dies in January. Mandela publicly announces that his son has died of AIDS complications.

2006: Publishes *Mandela: The Authorized Portrait*.

2007: Witnesses the installation of grandson Mandla Mandela as chief of the Mvezo Traditional Council.

2008: Turns ninety years old. Asks the emerging generations to continue the fight for social justice.

2009: Mandela's birthday, July 18, is endorsed by the United Nations as International Nelson Mandela Day.

2010: His great-granddaughter, Zenani Mandela, is killed in a car accident in June. Publishes *Conversations with Myself*.

2011: Publishes *Nelson Mandela by Himself*.

2012: Post-presidential office closed. Celebrates his ninety-fourth birthday.

Nelson Mandela played by Idris Elba

Idris Elba is a British television, theatre, and film actor who has starred in both British and American productions. He has worked in a variety of TV roles including *The Wire*, the American production of *The Office*, and the award-winning BBC show *Luther*, as well as starring in the films *The Losers*, *Takers*, *Thor*, *Prometheus*, and *Pacific Rim*. He has received awards for his roles in *Takers*, *The Losers*, and *Luther*, including a Golden Globe Award for Best Actor in *Luther*. He says playing Mandela was a complete honor for both him and his family. "His life is amazing, has been amazing, and continues to be. My parents are from West Africa—Sierra Leone and Ghana. My dad was very, very close to Mandela's story, and he always talked about him at home. When I told him I was playing Mandela in the film, he nearly burst into tears. Thank you, Madiba, from my family to yours. It is a privilege to play you in this film."

Teenage Mandela played by Atandwa Kani

Son of celebrated South African actor John Kani, Atandwa Kani was exposed to the entertainment industry at a young age. Kani plays the young Mandela between the ages of sixteen and his mid-twenties, a role he says being Xhosa [Mandela was also Xhosa] helped him prepare for. "The fact that I am Xhosa was really reassuring for me. I know the landscapes in the film; I have the environment that Mandela grew up in around me and in my memory. Being here and playing Madiba made me feel directly connected to the ancestors, and it is a privilege and an honor to be playing this great man's life and be part of all of this."

Winnie Mandela played by Naomie Harris

London-born Naomie Harris graduated with honors from Cambridge University in 1998 with a degree in social and political science. She received international recognition for her role as Tia Dalma/Calypso in *Pirates of the Caribbean: Dead Man's Chest* and *At World's End*, and has also starred in *Miami Vice*, *A Cock and Bull Story*, *Street Kings*, *The First Grader*, and the James Bond film, *Skyfall*. Harris considers it a rare opportunity for an actress to interpret such a multi-dimensional character. "Winnie is propelled from life as a young bride and mother to the harsh reality of being married to a political prisoner, abandoned with two young children. In order to survive she had to draw on an incredible strength. I can't imagine how it must have been for her; she was completely alone, there were no rules or regulations to save her; she was at the mercy of a brutal police force who acted with impunity to get at Mandela."

Walter Sisulu played by Tony Kgoroge

Tony Kgoroge is an award-winning South African theatre, television, and film actor and has starred in numerous films including *Skin*, *Blood Diamond*, *Lord of War*, *Hotel Rwanda*, *Hijack Stories*, *The Bird Can't Fly*, Clint Eastwood's *Invictus*, and *The First Grader* directed by Justin Chadwick. Kgoroge plays Nelson Mandela's long time comrade Walter Sisulu. He says playing the role of "Uncle Walter" was a great honour. "Mandela once told me, 'It's not me it's the team,' and I think that that idea came from Sisulu. He was the one who said to Mandela, 'When you're alone, you will not win. But when we're together, we're strong. And we can win.' This was a man who knew how to take care of a nation, take care of a family and take care of the others around him." In the film, Tony Kgoroge's wife, Sthandiwe Kgoroge, plays the role of Walter Sisulu's wife Albertina Sisulu, also a staunch ANC activist.

Ahmed Kathrada played by Riaad Moosa

Riaad Moosa is one of South Africa's most popular and acclaimed comics. Moosa says playing dedicated stalwart of the anti-apartheid struggle Ahmed Kathrada helped him better understand self-sacrifice, inner strength, and patience. "I was thirty-five years old when we filmed on Robben Island. This resonated for me as Kathy [as Ahmed Kathrada is affectionately known] was thirty-five when he was sent to Robben Island. One day on the boat trip back from the Island after shooting, I watched the Island fade into the distance. I was still thirty-five, and I was going home. Kathy was released from prison aged sixty. I asked him how one approaches the concept of life imprisonment. He said, 'I recall the Chinese proverb—I grumbled that I had no shoes, until I met a man with no feet.' He's a special man. They all are. When I grumble I have no shoes, I go to the shoe store."

Govan Mbeki played by Fana Mokoena

SAFTA award–winning South African actor Fana Mokoena motion picture credits include *Man on Ground*, *The Lab*, *Inside Story*, *Violence*, *Hotel Rwanda*, *Dangerous Ground*, *Jump the Gun*, *Inside*, *Machine Gun Preacher*, and *World War Z*. Mokoena plays Govan Mbeki, one of the six Rivonia Trialists imprisoned on Robben Island alongside Nelson Mandela. "One of the reasons I wanted to play Mbeki is that there's very little known about him, even though he was key, especially at Robben Island. He was seen as the elderly peacemaker, the guy who put the group together in a very sort of fatherly manner. I think the camaraderie between the seven on Robben Island is what made the story of Nelson Mandela. Madiba talks about how without his comrades he would not have achieved what he has; that everyday was literally about everybody else. It's the thing that got them through, every day."

Raymond Mhlaba played by Zolani Mkiva

Zolani Mkiva is a practitioner of one of the oldest oral traditions in South Africa: the *imbongi* or praise poet. Zolani rose to prominence in 1990 when as a schoolboy he was asked to praise the recently released Nelson Mandela at his "Welcome Home" rally in the Transkei, and went on to perform at Nelson Mandela's inauguration as president in 1994. Mkiva plays Raymond Mhlaba, one of the six Rivonia Trialists imprisoned on Robben Island alongside Nelson Mandela and is also the film's cultural advisor. He says the film is an important platform to tell South Africa's story. "Many people know that Nelson Mandela went to prison for twenty-seven years but don't know the detail of what he went through. This is an opportunity for us to tell the world of our struggle against the racism of apartheid as those who experienced it firsthand."

Andrew Mlangeni played by Simo Magwaza

SAFTA-nominated South African actor Simo Magwaza has starred in numerous local and international film and television productions and his films include *Hotel Rwanda*, *Red Tide*, *A Good Man in Africa*, *Beat the Drum*, *Platinum*, *Manhunters*, *The Good Provider*, and *District 9*. Magwaza says being part of a film about the life of the world's most famous prisoner and politician was a great honor. "To take part in a movie that tells of the struggle that we came from allows one to better understand the position the stalwarts found themselves in during those difficult times. It was a privilege to have played the role of Andrew Mlangeni, an incredible supporter of the struggle who was also best known as the friend of our icon, Madiba. Mlangeni was a quiet but effective comrade who dedicated his life to a free democratic country."

Elias Motsoaledi played by Thapelo Mokoena

Thapelo Mokoena is a South African actor and television presenter. Mokoena plays Elias Motsoaledi, one of the seven Rivonia Trialists imprisoned on Robben Island, and says being part of the film was life changing. "Being on Robben Island and re-living every moment through the lens was a truly humbling experience. I lost count of how many times I was close to tears during filming, realizing it was only a fraction of what our freedom fighters went through. My freedom as an artist and individual in South Africa came at a high price, and is one that cannot be measured."

Evelyn Mase played by Terry Pheto

South African actress Terry Pheto is best known for her leading role as Miriam in the 2005 Oscar-winning feature film *Tsotsi*. Pheto says portraying Mandela's first wife, Evelyn Mase, is easily the most meaningful role she has played so far. "The magnitude of playing the woman who helped mold the man who would carry the burden of a nation's destiny and subsequently change the course of our history, is not lost on me. Growing up in South Africa during a time of political turmoil where freedom was a distant thought, the soft whispers about a man who was fighting for our liberation kept me inspired that someday I would be able to live my own dream. Nelson Mandela has dedicated his life to fighting for a great cause and gave up everything, including his family, to fight for a better country for everyone. It is a privilege to be part of telling the story of the world's most recognized and loved icon, my hero."

Zindzi Mandela played by Lindiwe Matshikiza

The daughter of playwright, actor, and writer John Matshikiza, South African actress Lindiwe Matshikiza was born in England and came to South Africa when she was eight. Matshikiza plays Zindzi (Zindziswa) Mandela, the younger of Nelson and Winnie Mandela's two daughters, a role she says is a huge responsibility. "Not only are you trying to get into the shoes of that person who has such political and historical significance and is in the memory of generations of people, but also into those of a daughter who was longing for her father and wanting to take up the mantel. But it is a beautiful challenge to be able to replay history and feel part of it."

James Gregory played by Jamie Bartlett

Jamie Bartlett is a South African actor who has appeared in films *American Ninja 2*, *Red Dust*, and *Beyond Borders*, among others. Bartlett plays Warrant Officer James Gregory, who was one of Nelson Mandela's prison warders, and describes portraying Gregory's journey as special to play. "As the Xhosa-speaking jailor of the state's 'enemy number one,' Gregory and Mandela shared much of their lives in front of one another. When Madiba walked out of Victor Verster Prison to freedom he left Gregory a totally changed man. Gregory's humanity and the political philosophy of his state employers, were fundamentally challenged by his relationship, and later friendship, with Madiba."

Kobie Coetsee played by Deon Lotz

South African actor Deon Lotz plays Minister of Justice Kobie Coetsee, who led a series of meetings with Nelson Mandela while he was in prison. Lotz says he feels privileged to be part of an exceptional film about a great and iconic man who is loved the world over, and felt it was important to tell Coetsee's side of the story as honestly and impartially as possible. "While he operated within a system that was inhumane, I wanted to communicate his human side, and ensure that he was honored for his part in the negotiations."

President F. W. de Klerk played by Gys de Villiers

President F. W. de Klerk who announced Nelson Mandela's unconditional release from prison in 1990, is played by South African actor Gys de Villiers, a role de Villiers describes as a "magnificent acting challenge." "When we were shooting one could sense the focus, commitment, and joy of the entire crew of being part of telling Mandela's story. To play the Nobel Peace Prize winner, F. W. de Klerk, made me realize the enormity of what he undertook to give up power and implement democracy in South Africa."

Our film only tells the story of one man,
but South Africa's struggle for freedom
is the story of thousands of brave men and women,
all of whom suffered, many of whom died,
for a cause the world long believed to be hopeless.

We salute each one of them for their
selfless determination, dedication, and valor
in achieving the freedom we enjoy today.

The idea for this book started at Archbishop Tutu's eightieth birthday on November 7, 2011. I discussed the idea with Geoff Blackwell and Ruth Hobday. They were very excited about the possibility of the book, and here we are today. Thank you Geoff and Ruth, the book is more beautiful than I ever imagined.

To Graça Machel, Winnie Madikizela-Mandela, Zenani and Zindzi Mandela, and the greater Mandela family—thank you for your support.

To Kathy, without you we would be lost. Thank you for always being there when we had questions, for meeting the many people involved in the film, and, most importantly, for your selflessness, humility, and friendship.

To the Nelson Mandela Foundation—Achmat, Sello, Verne, and Sahm; thank you for all your support and assistance, and for sharing your archives with us.

To the Videovision Team—thank you for your support and commitment. All your efforts are most appreciated.

To Team Long Walk—thank you for the passion with which you worked on the film and for giving it your all.

Lastly, thank you to everyone who has been part of the journey of making this amazing motion picture. Together we have created a film which will tell the world Madiba's story for generations to come.

Anant Singh
Producer, *Mandela*

THE WEINSTEIN COMPANY, ANANT SINGH PRESENTS

IN ASSOCIATION WITH ORIGIN PICTURES, PATHÉ, DISTANT HORIZON,

INDUSTRIAL DEVELOPMENT CORPORATION OF SOUTH AFRICA AND NATIONAL EMPOWERMENT FUND A VIDEOVISION ENTERTAINMENT PRODUCTION

A JUSTIN CHADWICK FILM MANDELA IDRIS ELBA NAOMIE HARRIS TONY KGOROGE RIAAD MOOSA JAMIE BARTLETT LINDIWE MATSHIKIZA TERRY PHETO DEON LOTZ

MUSIC BY ALEX HEFFES MUSIC CONTRIBUTIONS CAIPHUS SEMENYA BLONDIE MAKHENE DIZU PLAATJIES DIRECTOR OF PHOTOGRAPHY LOL CRAWLEY EDITOR RICK RUSSELL

PRODUCTION DESIGNER JOHNNY BREEDT COSTUME DESIGNERS DIANA CILLIERS RUY FILIPE CASTING DIRECTOR MOONYEENN LEE CO-PRODUCERS ROBERT NAIDOO BRIAN COX VLOKKIE GORDON

EXECUTIVE PRODUCERS CAMERON MCCRACKEN FRANÇOIS IVERNEL GEOFFREY QHENA BASIL FORD SUDHIR PRAGJEE SANJEEV SINGH PHILISIWE MTHETHWA HLENGIWE MAKHATHINI

PRODUCER FOR ORIGIN PICTURES DAVID M. THOMPSON PRODUCED BY ANANT SINGH BASED ON 'LONG WALK TO FREEDOM' BY NELSON MANDELA SCREENPLAY BY WILLIAM NICHOLSON DIRECTED BY JUSTIN CHADWICK

© 2013 LONG WALK TO FREEDOM (PTY) LTD

Credits not contractual

159

BOOK PHOTOGRAPHIC SOURCES AND PERMISSIONS

Every effort has been made to trace the copyright holders of the images reproduced in this book and the publisher apologizes for any unintentional omission. We would be pleased to hear from any not acknowledged here and undertake to make all reasonable efforts to include the appropriate acknowledgment in any subsequent editions. Images not included below are film stills from *Mandela* and are copyright © 2013 Long Walk to Freedom (Pty) Ltd.

Page 5: Associated Press/Adil Bradlow; p. 7: Dana Gluckstein; p. 11: Johnny Breedt; pp. 26, 28: Duggan-Cronin Collection, McGregor Museum, Kimberley; p. 32: Howard Pim Library, University of Fort Hare; p. 33: Ahmed Kathrada/Herbert Shore; p. 35: Museum Africa; p. 37: (left) Museum Africa, (right) UWC Robben Island Museum Mayibuye Archive/Eli Weinberg; pp. 38, 41: (all) Bailey's African History Archives/Bob Gosani; p. 43: Elinor Sisulu/Sisulu Family; p. 45: (left and right) Jurgen Schadeberg; p. 51: (left and right) Jurgen Schadeberg; p. 57: (left and right) Robben Island Museum Mayibuye Archive/Eli Weinberg; p. 59: Jurgen Schadeberg; p. 61: (left) Robben Island Museum Mayibuye Archive/Eli Weinberg, (right) Museum Africa; p. 63: Robben Island Museum Mayibuye Archive/Eli Weinberg; p. 65: Historical Papers Research Archives, The Library, University of Witswatersrand; p. 69: Historical Papers Research Archives, The Library, University of Witswatersrand; p. 70: JonCom Publications; p. 72: Bailey's African History Archives/Alf Kumalo; p. 74: Nelson Mandela Centre of Memory at the Nelson Mandela Foundation, courtesy Palace of Justice, Pretoria; pp. 77, 79: Historical Papers Research Archives, The Library, University of Witswatersrand; p. 81: (left and right) South African National Archives; pp. 84–85: Robben Island Museum/Matthew Willman; pp. 86–87: (left) Cloete Breytenbach /Daily Express London, (right) Matthew Willman; p. 88: Robben Island Museum/Matthew Willman; p. 91: Cloete Breytenbach/Daily Express London; p. 103: Nelson Mandela Centre of Memory at the Nelson Mandela Foundation/Nelson Mandela papers; p. 104: Robben Island Museum Mayibuye Archive/Eli Weinberg; p. 108: Bailey's African History Archives/Mike Mzeleni; p. 112: photographer unknown; p. 113: (all) South African History Archives, courtesy Historical Papers, University of the Witwatersrand Library; p. 121: (left) Morris Zwi; p. 125: (top and bottom left, bottom right) Guy Tillim, (top right) Corbis/Gideon Mendel; p. 127: Corbis/Gideon Mendel; pp. 128–29: Robben Island Museum Mayibuye Archive/DAF Collection; p. 134: Graeme Williams; pp. 136–37: Africa Media Online/Chris Ledochowski; pp. 138–39: Picturenet Africa/Ken Oosterbroek; p. 147: photographer unknown; p. 150: Gallo Images/Paul Weinberg; p. 151: Corbis/David Turnley; p. 156: (Nelson Mandela, color image) Michael Crabtree/Reuters; (Nelson Mandela, black and white image) Howard Pim Library, University of Fort Hare; (Winnie Mandela) Graeme Williams/The Bigger Picture; (Walter Sisulu) Bailey's African History Archives/Bob Gosani; (Govan Mbeki) Bailey's African History Archives; (Raymond Mhlaba) Mhlaba Family Col., courtesy Liliesleaf Trust; (Andrew Mlangeni) courtesy Historical Papers Research Archives, UWL; p. 157: (Elias Motsoaledi) courtesy Historical Papers Research Archives, UWL; (Evelyn Mase) Elinor Sisulu/Sisulu Family; (Zindzi Mandela) Morris Zwi; (Kobie Coetsee) South African National Archives, courtesy Nelson Mandela Foundation; (F. W. de Klerk) Gerard Julien/AFP.

BOOK ACKNOWLEDGMENTS

The publisher would like to thank all those who have contributed to *Mandela—A Film and Historical Companion* and, along with the people and organizations mentioned in this section, we would particularly like to thank the following for their help in compiling the book: Ahmed Kathrada; Sahm Venter, Lucia Raadschelders, Sello Hatang, and Verne Harris of the Nelson Mandela Centre of Memory; Anant Singh and Nilesh Singh of Videovision Entertainment.

The publisher is grateful for literary permissions to reproduce those items below subject to copyright. Every effort has been made to trace the copyright holders and the publisher apologizes for any unintentional omission. We would be pleased to hear from any not acknowledged here and undertake to make all reasonable efforts to include the appropriate acknowledgment in any subsequent editions.

Page 18 and throughout the book: quoted material from *Long Walk to Freedom* reprinted by kind permission of Nelson R. Mandela; pp. 23, 28, 41, 45, 51, 61, 82, 123, 133, and 143: quoted material from the screenplay *Mandela* by William Nicholson reprinted by permission of Long Walk to Freedom (Pty) Ltd; p. 26 and throughout the book: quoted material from Nelson Mandela's interviews, speeches, and writings (unless otherwise specified) reprinted by kind permission of Nelson R. Mandela and the Nelson Mandela Foundation; pp. 32, 37, 57, 96, 98, 103, 107, and 130: quoted material taken from *Conversations with Myself*; pp. 46, 63, 65, 69, 71, 74, 77, 88, 92, 113, 128, 145, and 149: quoted material taken from *Nelson Mandela by Himself: The Authorised Book of Quotations*; p. 63: Ahmed Kathrada, excerpt from the *Independent* (South Africa), July 11, 1998, reprinted by permission of Ahmed Kathrada; pp. 73, 74, 77, 87, 90, 101, 114, 120, 137, and 150: quoted material from *Mandela: The Authorised Portrait*, reprinted by kind permission of Nelson R. Mandela and the Nelson Mandela Foundation; p. 147: quoted material from *No Future without Forgiveness* by Desmond M. Tutu, reprinted by permission of Desmond Tutu.

SELECT BIBLIOGRAPHY

Mandela, Nelson, *Conversations with Myself*, Macmillan Publishers, London, 2010

Mandela, Nelson, *Long Walk to Freedom*, Little, Brown and Company, London, 1994

Mandela, Nelson, *Nelson Mandela by Himself: The Authorised Book of Quotations*, Macmillan Publishers, London, 2011

Nicol, Mike, *Mandela: The Authorised Portrait*, PQ Blackwell, Auckland, 2006

Tutu, Desmond, *No Future without Forgiveness*, Doubleday, New York, 1999

First published in the United States in 2013 by Chronicle Books LLC.

First produced and originated in 2013 by PQ Blackwell Limited
116 Symonds Street, Auckland 1010, New Zealand
www.pqblackwell.com

Library of Congress Cataloging-in-Publication Data available.

ISBN: 978-1-4521-2841-2

Manufactured in China

Designed by Bridget White

10 9 8 7 6 5 4 3 2 1

Chronicle Books LLC
680 Second Street
San Francisco, California 94107
www.chroniclebooks.com

PQ Blackwell
Publisher: Geoff Blackwell
Editor-in-Chief: Ruth Hobday
Editor: Jo Garden
Additional editorial and research: Rachel Clare